Don't Give UP!

You Can Be Your Own Therapist

Don't Give UP!

You Can Be Your Own Therapist

CATHERINE WORD BURTON
M.A.,LPC-LMFT

KUDU

Acknowledgments

Special thanks to the following people:

Deb Hinton, for entering my thoughts into the computer as I spoke and for the many hours of listening to me describe counseling sessions as we recreated the scenarios clients would experience.

John Smith, for offering your writing expertise and computer-processing skills.

Jennifer Strickland, for teaching me so many basic fundamentals of writing and adding my input into the computer. Your insights helped shape the content of what the readers should know about the techniques used in the therapeutic process.

Kathy R. Green, for your divine insights, expert guidance and straight-forward direction. You caught the vision and brought it to fulfillment, I will be eternally grateful.

Barry Burton, for spending endless amounts of time entering script into the computer.

Rileigh King, for entering corrections into the computer.

My clients, most of all, for 20 years of on-the-job instruction that taught me far and above what any formal education could have. You are the backbone of this book, and what I have learned from you is immeasurable.

Mary Anne Watson PhD, Intern Supervisor, and much more, for the privilege of studying and learning from your brilliant mind and innovative techniques. Clinical director at Charter Hospital.

Art Arauzo, MD, Medical Director, Charter Hospital, for sharing your knowledge of psychotropic medications and therapeutic expertise that has given me an immense advantage in diagnosing pathology.

Teddie Bryant for her generosity.

Lanelle Young for her editing expertise.

Contents

Introduction

Have you ever felt like "giving up" on your marriage or your relationship? Maybe you are tired of going round and round and getting nowhere. Perhaps you and your spouse have drifted so far apart that you hardly know each other anymore, and you're wondering if it will be worth the effort to continue.

You may want to make things work, but you don't know how. Don't give up—do your due diligence—there is still a chance!

When couples come into my office, they have a lot of pain and hurt. They are angry and resentful. They feel cheated. This isn't what they signed up for. When they married, they had a dream of building a life together. They began with high hopes of living out this dream. It's a deep heartbreak when these things don't work out.

Wouldn't you want to find out what has gone wrong, and learn what you can do about it? Wouldn't you want a chance to get your dream back?

As you read this book you will see actual events and the therapeutic interventions that were used in a series of sessions with three couples as they worked together with Dr. Carla Brightman (a pseudonym). I'm offering you a front row seat to their ups and downs. You may closely relate to their anger, frustration, doubts and fears. They're all included in the stories related in this book. As you experience their emotional journeys, you can also rejoice with them and celebrate their progress and recovery. You may even see yourself in their situations and learn from their struggles. You can apply this same wisdom in your own personal relationship. So, don't give up! Apply the skills and advice in this book and <u>become your own therapist</u>. You can do it!

The Chambers

CHAPTER 1

Lines Have Been Crossed

Everyone has experienced unwelcome intruders into their personal lives; those who always think they know what is best, and how they should live their lives. As you read this chapter you may realize that some of this applies to you. You may have someone in your life this matches. It's easy to be blindsided by the various types of manipulation and schemes these intruders use to put themselves in positions of influence. Follow Tamara and Kyle to see how they rebalanced the boundary equation and negotiated freedom from domination in their personal lives.

Tinderbox Marriage

Kyle Chambers had been on a "low boil" since early in his marriage to Tamara. However, he felt that his mother-in-law, JoAnn, had recently redoubled her efforts to sabotage their home life, especially since his wife had become pregnant. Tension was escalating, and Kyle wasn't coping well with the rising stress, which was now spilling over into his work. People at work were beginning to notice Kyle's sharp tone of voice and lack of patience over the usual problems encountered in managing a commercial building project. His current furniture store construction project was soon due for a major inspection by corporate heads. He needed to get some relief from this on-going war on the home front, before serious consequences erupted in his marriage or in his work, or both.

He and Tamara had been married eighteen months when she learned she was pregnant. Tamara was teaching second grade and modeling on the side for local fashion shows at *Mon Chez Moi,* a large, upscale department store. It's where her mother, JoAnn, worked as the store's fashion marketing manager. Kyle was aware that JoAnn's domineering personality had always overshadowed Tamara. Although JoAnn's interference in their relationship had been present from the start, it seemed that her intrusions into their family life had grown exponentially, to the point that he now found it to be intolerable.

Tamara found contentment teaching young children, but JoAnn had insisted that she continue modeling at Mon Chez Moi's couture showings and charity auction shows "to keep her hand in." JoAnn had always lived vicariously through Tamara. When Tamara was a child, JoAnn entered her into beauty pageants and auditioned her with modeling agencies and advertising jobs. Tamara really didn't enjoy the fussy attention but was always eager to please her mother.

When Tamara told JoAnn that she was expecting a baby, JoAnn was thrilled. She immediately began planning her grandchild's nursery, down to the most minute detail. Her encroachments continued with efforts to tell Tamara how to handle her pregnancy and diet, which her daughter initially seemed to appreciate. Without asking, JoAnn signed Tamara up for a prenatal yoga class that automatically rolled into a post-delivery mommy/baby yoga class. As usual, Tamara went along with her mom's suggestion. JoAnn also insisted on going to Tamara's obstetric appointments. Though neither Kyle nor Tamara ever asked

JoAnn for this support, she was determined to intrude. When Kyle complained about it, Tamara lectured him about being ungrateful for the help.

Therefore, JoAnn was there with Kyle and his wife to hear the baby's first heartbeat, see the first sonogram, and learn that they were expecting a girl. A couple of weeks later, JoAnn bought an entire wardrobe for the baby in pinks, lace, and ruffles and began pushing Tamara to name the baby Chelsea. JoAnn explained that "Chelsea Chambers" sounded like a great professional name for a model/pageant contestant. Kyle wasn't surprised when Tamara capitulated to her mother's wishes yet again. The hair on Kyle's neck and arms stood up as he listened to them argue over the name, while JoAnn reinforced her opinion. When he could stomach it no longer, he turned on his heel, stomped out of the house and went for a drive.

During the next few months, Tamara continued experiencing morning sickness. This was JoAnn's cue to overrule the doctor's advice regarding diet, weight, and exercise. She monitored practically every move Tamara made. Tamara accommodated her mother's requests as well as she could, but it was clear that Tamara wasn't enjoying her pregnancy.

Tamara suddenly experienced unexpected complications during her seventh month. After examination, her gynecologist, Dr. Grayson, felt it was necessary to schedule Tamara for a caesarean section the very next day. Kyle remembered feeling confused and frightened. Tamara was terrified and called her mother from the car with the news.

Kyle wished Tamara hadn't made that call. Of course, when they arrived home, JoAnn came over immediately to spend the night. Kyle was dreading the inevitable again; he knew JoAnn would dominate the entire situation. He had expected to feel a myriad of emotions at the birth of his daughter—joy and excitement at the least—but not frustration, fear, and dread!

Baby Chelsea was delivered via C-section the next morning, weighing four pounds, two ounces and appearing healthy. However, soon after the baby arrived at the NICU, she began having respiratory difficulties that required treatment and supervision. She also experienced some digestive complications, which required a special formula for the newborn's sensitive system. Though her pediatrician explained that Chelsea was not in imminent danger, the baby remained in the hospital during the next week while her progress was monitored. Kyle was beside himself, worrying about his wife and daughter.

He was not surprised when JoAnn immediately took an extended leave of absence in order to be available to help her daughter and granddaughter. He had to admit that he was initially relieved by the way JoAnn carefully studied the guidelines the doctor provided for Chelsea's care and seemed prepared to handle any unexpected situation.

In the meantime, Tamara experienced a delayed recovery with complications from the C-section, resulting in a few extra days in the hospital. While Tamara and the baby were still admitted, JoAnn moved into the house to be available the minute Tamara was discharged. She wanted to have everything ready and perfect for the baby when they came home. When they were finally released, JoAnn accompanied Kyle and Tamara home. Tamara was obviously thankful that JoAnn was there to take over. And take over, she did!

Kyle noticed that the very thought of her mother leaving for any amount of time caused Tamara to fret and grow frantic. Though Tamara had told him that she looked forward to their lives returning to a normal pace and that she missed teaching, it was clear to him that she didn't feel confident about handling Chelsea on her own. Chelsea still had trouble sleeping for more than a couple of hours at a time and cried a lot.

Though Tamara's recovery from the C-section progressed, her emotional state deteriorated. She was depressed, lethargic, and prone to crying jags. Even worse, she seemed terrified of Chelsea. Her fears of accidentally harming Chelsea practically immobilized Tamara. Of course, JoAnn was only too happy to step into the role as Chelsea's primary caregiver. JoAnn also took extra measures to pamper Tamara, anticipating and indulging her daughter's every noticeable need.

Kyle became concerned over Tamara's behavior and insisted on going with her to her last appointment with Dr. Grayson. When the doctor questioned her about her progress, she began to sob uncontrollably.

"I don't know what's wrong with me, Dr. Grayson! I can't figure out what I need to do to get out of this slump. I don't trust myself with Chelsea. She seems so fragile, and I feel so inadequate!" Tamara cried. "I think I must be going crazy!"

Dr. Grayson tried to comfort her. "Tamara, you're not going crazy. It sounds like you're experiencing symptoms of postpartum depression, a rather common problem in new mothers as their hormones are rebalancing. Since you're not breastfeeding, I'm going to prescribe an antidepressant. This is a low dose and should help you feel better in about a week or two. If you're still struggling after that, I'll recommend a counselor to give you some additional support.".

After returning from the doctor, Tamara immediately went to JoAnn in utter despair, sharing Dr. Grayson's assessment of her condition. "I don't know if I'll ever be able to take care of my daughter, Mother. I must be a horrible mom!" Tamara whined. "I could never make it without you."

Kyle audibly groaned at Tamara's words. JoAnn's presence and determination had overshadowed any acknowledgement of his role as a new father. He felt invisible and more out of the loop than ever.

Joann watched him closely anytime he was around Chelsea. He couldn't pick Chelsea up without it turning into a "teaching moment." So, in the following weeks, as Tamara's mood improved, Kyle mustered his courage. One evening he told Tamara it was past time for JoAnn to move back to her home. Tamara fretted that her mother would feel unappreciated for all the help she'd given them. She was also concerned that stressing JoAnn with a hasty exodus would trigger her mother's chronic asthma. Kyle refused to back down, and after complaining bitterly, Tamara gave in.

"So, I suppose it's going to be my dirty little job, telling Mother to leave. Right, Kyle?" Tamara yelled at him.

"Well, I could tell her, but you can imagine how that would go!" Kyle snarled back.

Tamara braced herself for the task, and after a very emotional exchange, JoAnn packed her things, sobbing, "You really don't appreciate all that I've done for you! I've tried my very best to be helpful to you both and to be a good Mimi to Chelsea, but the more I do, the more the two of you seem to resent me. I don't understand how you can treat me like this!" JoAnn screeched, glaring at Kyle.

Choking on her tears, JoAnn dissolved into a coughing fit as she panted to her car. She draped herself weakly over the steering wheel for a moment, then squealed her tires in protest as she drove away. Tamara became hysterical at the sight and began shrieking at Kyle.

"See what you've made me do! You've handled this all wrong! Now Mother is hurt and upset. She'll probably go into a full-blown asthma attack! Did you hear that cough? I could hear her coughing all the way to the car! She should be feeling our gratitude, not our disloyalty." Tamara paced back and forth on the front porch, chewing her already short nails.

Once again, Kyle found himself caught in the middle and labeled as the villain. "Tamara, can't you see how she manipulates you? JoAnn is faking those coughing spasms. I wouldn't be surprised to see her nominated for an Oscar," Kyle shouted. "She's just using her asthma as an excuse to manipulate you to do whatever she wants and to make you feel guilty! It's happened so many times now, I can't even count them.

There is one too many people in this marriage. Maybe I should be the one to leave, instead of JoAnn."

"You are being completely ridiculous—you don't understand!" Tamara screamed at him through her tears. "I love both of you, and this puts me right in the middle, between you and Mother. No matter what I do, somebody's going to be upset. I can't win in this situation, and now everyone's unhappy! You'll never stop, will you? You must really hate her."

"Okay, great. I'm always getting the blame! This is never going to end, is it?" Kyle spat out the words.

Feeling depleted, Tamara walked away and spent the night in Chelsea's room. She slept fitfully, hoping Chelsea wouldn't cry and that everything would be all right. About midnight she was startled awake by her cell phone ringing.

"What, Mother? I can't hear you. The phone woke Chelsea, and now she's fussing. You're where? The emergency room! Oh, no, no. No, it's fine, Mother! I'll be there as soon as I can get dressed," Tamara cried.

"Kyle! Wake up! Mother's in the hospital! She had an asthma attack! I just knew this was going to happen. I need you to feed Chelsea and see if you can get her back to sleep. I've got to check on Mother at the hospital," Tamara shouted as she thrust the squirming infant at him.

Kyle already knew that if JoAnn had been in real danger, someone from the hospital would have called, rather than JoAnn herself. But there would be no point in trying to convince his wife of that.

We can't get rid of JoAnn for even a few hours, can we? he thought to himself. While he was glad JoAnn had been "evicted," he was anxious over his decision. He wondered whether he had pulled the plug on JoAnn's presence too soon. It was clear that Tamara was still feeling anxious and insecure about managing Chelsea's care.

Shortly after Tamara arrived at the emergency room, JoAnn was waiting. She had already received a respiratory treatment and was awaiting release. Tamara insisted that her mother come home with her so that she could watch over her to be sure JoAnn didn't have another attack. Kyle wasn't surprised when the two of them walked into the house together about 2 a.m., and Tamara apologized profusely for her mother's asthma attack.

"Wow, JoAnn, you certainly seem to have regained your strength quickly!" Kyle growled, gritting his teeth "What did they give you at the hospital? Must have been something potent!".

"I'm surprised to hear all that concern in your voice," JoAnn snapped, glaring at him. "Where's the baby? Is she alright?"

"Mother, don't worry about Chelsea. We'll take care of her. You just need to lie down and get some rest now," Tamara fussed.

And so, JoAnn was back underfoot again. Kyle was livid but realized that saying anything more would only escalate the situation. "Why don't you just go back to bed? I'm going to read for a while," he sighed.

"After all I've been through, I'm wide awake now," JoAnn announced.

So, while Tamara and JoAnn sat at the breakfast table, JoAnn began to spell out her plan to make herself indispensable. "I know how much you've missed teaching, so maybe it's time you thought about going back to work. Besides it's high time you got out of the house for a while. I'm afraid you'll just get depressed again, hanging around here. Since it's obviously an inconvenience for me to stay here, I could keep Chelsea for you during the day at my house, so you and Kyle can get back into a routine. I'd be glad to come pick her up in the mornings before you go to work."

"You're right. I do miss teaching and would like to get back to it," Tamara agreed, "but I'm not sure if I'm ready yet. Let me have a little time to think about your offer. And frankly, I would feel guilty about putting so much responsibility for Chelsea's care back on you again." Tamara was clearly torn.

"Not to worry. I know her schedule and routine, and I'm comfortable with managing that," JoAnn assured.

"Let's not get ahead of ourselves, Mother. I'm still pretty worried about you. That seemed like a pretty bad asthma attack you had... You know these things always get worse at night, and I really think you should just stay over for a few days until we're sure you're out of the woods."

"Well, you have a point. I'm still wheezing and coughing and having difficulty catching my breath at times," JoAnn suppressed a smile.

"Maybe it's for the best." Tamara was still questioning herself and felt anxious without her mother's presence. JoAnn always knew what to do.

When Kyle got home the next evening, he rushed in and pulled his wife aside, demanding, "What is she still doing here?"

Tamara grabbed his arm and pulled him into the bedroom. "Shhhhh, Kyle! She'll hear you! I asked her to stay. She's still wheezing and coughing, and I don't want her to have to go back to the hospital. I want to make sure she is stabilized on her new medication. A few more days isn't going to matter," she explained anxiously as he stared at her in disbelief.

"Have you lost your mind? We finally got her out of here." Kyle shouted explosively. "You're such a fool, Tamara! You always fall for her manipulations. I'm just going to pack a bag and stay at a hotel until she leaves. I'm through with this!" As he started to gather his things, he realized that, once again, JoAnn was a step ahead of him and had already executed her next maneuver in their lives.

"I'll call you when I get settled in and let you know where I am," Kyle yelled as he snatched his keys from the table and stormed out the door, duffle bag in hand.

JoAnn was aware of the commotion but stayed out of the way until she heard the door slam. She emerged from Chelsea's room to find her daughter in tears. "What in the world is happening?" she demanded, acting surprised.

"Oh, Kyle is just being a jerk!"Tamara cried. "He didn't even give me a chance to explain anything. He just packed his bag and ran out the door. He's staying at a hotel tonight. That's fine with me. I don't need this stress!"

"Oh, I'm so sorry, Sweetie—"JoAnn broke off and flew into another coughing fit. "I'll just sit down for a minute until I can catch my breath. Then I'll prepare us something for dinner."

Meanwhile, Kyle kicked off his shoes and flopped onto the hotel bed. "Wow! I shouldn't have to leave my own home," he fumed. He picked up the TV remote, poured himself a stiff drink from the minibar, and clicked mindlessly through the channels. As he began to calm down a bit, he thought about Mark, a friend from work who was seeing a counselor, and decided to call him to get the doctor's name and phone number first thing in the morning. He couldn't see any way out of this. He and Tamara had gone round and round about JoAnn countless times, with no solution in sight. Better try to get some professional assistance before he lost more than his temper. Kyle felt so powerless and knew his marriage was in jeopardy. He feared that his anger might provoke him in ways he would later regret.

Kyle's fingers were trembling the next morning as he dialed the number of the counselor Mark had given him. "Brighter Day Counseling Services. This is Dr. Carla Brightman. How can I help you?" "Dr. Brightman, My name is Kyle Chambers. I'm so glad I reached you. I'm at the end of my rope. My wife and I are under a tremendous amount of strain," Kyle's voice shook as he spoke. "I'm afraid we could be headed for a divorce."

"Well, I'm glad you called me, Kyle. This sounds serious!" Dr. Brightman observed.

"Um. I'd like to make an appointment. I think we're at the breaking point," Kyle stated, stress cracking his voice.

"I'll try to get you in as soon as possible!"

"Yes, please, Doctor, I'm ready to explode. Do you have anything available on Tuesday afternoon? My schedule's usually light on Tuesdays," he added.

"Sure. How about 2:00 p.m. on Tuesday, then?"

"It's on my calendar. Thanks so much, Dr. Brightman. See you then."

Exposing the Rottweiler

Tuesday afternoon couldn't have arrived a minute too soon for Kyle. He entered Dr. Brightman's office fifteen minutes early. She greeted him and gave him some forms to fill out. When he finished, she ushered him into her office. "Did you have any trouble finding the office, Mr. Chambers?"

"No problems getting here. And please, call me Kyle," he replied nervously.

"Is this your first time to see a counselor?" "Yes, it is. The truth is, I never thought I'd have to contact someone like you. I always thought we should figure things out on our own," Kyle added with disbelief.

"I'm sure you've tried your best, and it sounded like you had hit a block when we talked the other day. This has got to be very nerve-rattling for you."

"I know I've got to get some help with this, as awkward as it is," Kyle admitted sheepishly. "I really don't like talking about my personal problems, especially to a perfect stranger."

"I hear that a lot. Most people feel the same way. So, on the phone you mentioned that you and your wife were having problems and that you felt like you were at the end of your rope. Tell me what's been going on."

"That's just it; I'm worn out. My home doesn't feel like it's my home anymore. As a matter of fact, I left a couple of nights ago and I'm staying in a hotel. It's my mother-in-law: she's in the middle of my home and marriage, and now she's taking over the parenting of our baby daughter. I mean, she's been staying there to help out since the baby was born, and she never leaves. JoAnn has always had a lot of control over my wife, Tamara. I thought that once we were married that would change, but no such luck! You wouldn't believe this woman, Dr. Brightman. Lately, it's become completely intolerable," Kyle complained. "Then I thought, 'Okay, things will change when Tamara becomes a mother,' but in fact, she's gotten much worse. She depends on JoAnn now more than ever." He sighed and pinched the area between his eyebrows, trying to ease the headache he felt coming on.

"Is this really necessary? Is your wife incapacitated in some way?"

"Let's just say that Tamara has been indoctrinated to believe that she's helpless without her mother's constant approval," Kyle explained. "Of course, it didn't help that Tamara has been diagnosed with something called postpartum depression, and JoAnn played heavily on her insecurities to work herself even more deeply into Tamara's life."

"Sounds like you're stuck in a classic 'Catch-22 situation.' You lose no matter what, right? Where would you like to go with this?" the doctor questioned.

"Well, I want to get rid of this interloper! Tamara and I have never been able to have the kind of marriage I would like because JoAnn overwhelms her and interferes in everything. Unfortunately, my wife seems to be more connected to her mother than she is to me. But she doesn't see it that way. I'm the outsider here!" Kyle blurted in exasperation.

"I'm sure it just feels normal to Tamara to cater to her mother. You said that she's been like this since her childhood. So, she obviously doesn't see the issue the way you do. This is a common boundary violation. Her mother definitely seems to be intrusive, and we'll have to help

Tamara realize how out of order this is. If she can understand this, she may be willing to rebalance her relationship with you and her mother."

"I don't know. I have no idea how to go about doing this. I love Tamara, and I don't want a divorce, but I can't imagine going on like this!"

"Do you think Tamara would be willing to come in with you and discuss this?"

"I believe that's going to be our only hope for turning things in the right direction. Our marriage is much too crowded with JoAnn in it."

"Let's try to sort this out," "Tell Tamara what we talked about here today and ask her to join you in a session. You've taken an important first step by coming. If you can convince Tamara to join us, we can begin working on this problem together. Hopefully, I'll hear from you soon. Good luck, Kyle."

Kyle left Dr. Brightman's office, hoping he hadn't just opened a Pandora's box that couldn't be shut again. But he was on a mission to save his marriage.

Indeed, Kyle did have a mission. Convincing his wife they needed professional help wouldn't be easy, especially since the core of their issue involved the volatile subject of Tamara's mother.

Kyle knew he had to get down to business and went straight home. He got right to the point. "Sit down, Tamara. We need to talk privately," Kyle directed, setting his jaw. "Is the Rottweiler still here?" "If you're referring to Mother, she's gone to the store! How rude of you to insult her that way!" A knot began to form in Tamara's stomach. She settled into her favorite chair, tucking her feet into the side of the seat. "She'll be back before long. What do you want?" she asked icily.

"You know we can't go on like this any longer. I saw a counselor today and told her that this situation with your mother is intolerable for me."

"What? You did what? You saw a counselor? This really puts me in a terrible position."

"Well, Tamara, as it's clear that we can't figure this out on our own; we're going to need some professional help to sort through it all. You know, Dr. Brightman seemed very understanding, and you need to join me in a session with her, as soon as possible. Getting some help from a professional is the only way I can see to work through this," Kyle asserted.

"So, you're willing to go to a complete stranger to figure out our family problems? She doesn't even know my mother. I won't have a complete stranger throwing Mother under the bus! That's just not going to happen." Tamara felt like a trapped animal. *No matter what I do here, I'm going to lose,* she thought desperately, twisting her hands as the silence stretched out between them. She was acutely aware that she was on the edge of losing either her husband or her mother, and she really had no choice but to seek help. She dreaded hearing what the counselor would expect of her, and felt her anxiety mounting at the very suggestion.

Kyle's frustration flushed his face and erupted in his voice. "You know, it's pretty clear that you're more worried about your mother's feelings than you are about our marriage. Either you come with me to the counselor, or our marriage has no chance!" he snapped, starting abruptly for the door.

Tamara was in tears now, sobbing hysterically, as she ran after him. "That sounded like a threat, Kyle! You don't just give me an ultimatum like that and take off! Don't you care what this is doing to me? Don't you see how you're tearing me apart?"

"I've said all I have to say on the subject," Kyle yelled back at her. "Let me know what you decide to do. I'm not going to wait much longer for you to make up your mind. Until you do, I'm staying at the hotel."

That night Tamara tossed and turned, and when she finally rose from her sleepless bed the next morning, she knew what she had to do. She marched stiffly into the kitchen and left Kyle a bitter-sounding voicemail, "Okay, Kyle. You win! Go ahead and call that counselor for an appointment. It looks like you're giving me no choice."

When Kyle got her message, he texted back: "Well, you finally got the picture. I'll make an appointment as soon as possible."

Exposing the Skeleton in the Closet

Kyle called the counselor immediately, and Tamara's nerves went raw when she learned an emergency session had been set up for them. The next day, they sat on opposite sides of Dr. Brightman's waiting room.

Tamara had bitten her nails down to the quick. She was fuming over being coerced into coming there, but she couldn't think of a way out. She'd considered every excuse she could manufacture but realized Kyle was in no mood to hear her. She loved him and didn't want to end up divorced and raising a child alone. Her mother had done that. Glaring across the room at her husband, she thought Kyle looked smug, as if he had already won the first round of this fight by simply getting her into this office. After a brief wait, Dr. Brightman called them in and greeted them.

"Thank you for coming in. Please make yourselves comfortable." Kyle sat in a chair, and Tamara seated herself on the far end of the couch away from him. Each of them sat rigidly, their arms crossed. Tension lined their faces.

"As you must know, Kyle came in to see me last week," Dr. Brightman began. "I know you are both having a hard time, and I really want to hear your side of the story. What do you think is going on, Tamara?" Tamara's eyes brimmed with tears as she squeezed a squishy stress ball. "It's just not fair! I'm stuck between my mother and Kyle. Mother wants to help us, although she does go overboard sometimes. I understand that. But it's affecting our marriage, and Kyle is constantly complaining. He's making me miserable. He's very angry, and he makes it so obvious in front of Mother. He's been so harsh with her, and I don't think he understands how devoted and grateful I am to her. Dr. Brightman, she raised me alone after she and Dad divorced. Dad remarried, and I didn't see him much after that. Mother made sure of it. She kept as much distance as possible between Dad and me, and she resented any attempts he made to contact me. He finally gave in. So, it's just been Mother and me for most of my life. She gave me every possible advantage. Her focus has always been on what she thought was best for me, so cutting Mother off from me is like cutting off a part of myself. And she's been such a help with Chelsea—I don't think I could have made it without her!" Tamara's lips trembled, revealing her deep dependency on her mother.

Kyle looked stunned. "Tamara, enough is enough. You need to grow up!"

"Kyle, you're always so angry with Mother that I can never talk to you about anything regarding her!" Tamara countered. "You'll never understand."

Dr. Brightman looked to Kyle. "Wow! What are you hearing, Kyle?" "What I hear is that we're stuck in the past." Kyle blurted. "Tamara, you sound pathetic! You still act like a child. I thought that you would start to feel more confident over time. But instead, you become more and more dependent on JoAnn, not less."

"Is that what you meant, Tamara—that you feel so dependent and helpless?"

"Well, that's not what I meant to say, but I guess it did sound that way," Tamara replied.

"That's very revealing," Dr. Brightman responded. "That's what we're here to sort out. Now, let's back up for a second, so I can point something out to you. Tamara, do you see that your only role model for motherhood is JoAnn? From what you said, she didn't want your father to have any influence in your life. It appears that she's trying to recreate that old pattern. She's trying to cut Kyle off from you and Chelsea, just as she did with you and your father. Does that feel familiar?"

A deafening silence pervaded the room as Tamara and Kyle both found themselves at a loss for words.

Dr. Brightman spoke soothingly, "It's obvious that there are very intense feelings on both sides of this issue. It clearly goes a lot deeper than either of you realized. That's why situations like this are so difficult: there's a lot more going on beneath the surface. It's clear that neither of you can develop in your role as husband and wife nor as parents as long as JoAnn is taking charge. The key lies in finding a solution that doesn't completely cut off JoAnn from her granddaughter but limits her influence and role in your lives. In other words, you'll need to set appropriate boundaries with her."

Dr. Brightman paused to see if they were following, and took a sip of water before going on, "Let me continue. What you are describing is an obvious boundary issue with JoAnn. We will have to renegotiate the boundaries with JoAnn. Let me explain. Boundaries are about setting appropriate limits and are different from walls. Walls completely shut people out, and that's not what we want to do. We will need to determine appropriate boundaries with JoAnn and come up with a compromise. We will assess how much involvement from JoAnn is appropriate versus how much is interference.

"Kyle mentioned to me that you suffered from postpartum depression, and as a result, Tamara, you have given your mother so much responsibility in caring for Chelsea. When, for one reason or another, we cannot take charge of our own lives, remember—someone else will. Nature abhors a vacuum, and someone or something will fill it!

"So, let's look at this. The best approach right now would be for each of you to have one or two individual sessions before we move forward with you as a couple. I hear your fears and concerns, Tamara, and I'll help you work on those. Kyle, I also hear your anger and frustration, and we'll work on that, as well. What do you think of this plan?"

Tamara took a deep breath and answered, "I'm relieved to learn that I don't have to completely sever my relationship with Mother. Thank you for that. I feel like I'm being torn apart!"

"Well, in a way you are. Would you be willing to come back for an individual session?

"Yeah, I think I need to talk more about this—without Kyle," Tamara responded.

"What about you, Kyle?" the doctor inquired. "Are you still staying at the hotel?"

"Uh, yeah. I'm not coming home again until JoAnn leaves," he asserted.

"You know, Dr. Brightman, he badly blew this out of proportion," Tamara added. "Mother had a very serious asthma attack just a few nights ago and had to go to the ER. Her new medication isn't working that well yet, so I don't want to send her home until I'm sure she's stabilized."

"So, here's what needs to happen," Dr. Brightman explained. "JoAnn should make an appointment with her physician as soon as possible to evaluate her progress with the new medication. Then, maybe you'll feel comfortable enough to let her go home again."

"Well, okay," Tamara sighed, though the knot in her stomach was still there.

"What about you, Kyle? Can you come in for an individual session, as well?"

"Well, sure, but I hope this won't go on much longer," he answered reluctantly.

Dr. Brightman nodded, "I understand, and I want you to know that we're going to focus on solution here, and not just dwell on the problems. We need to get a structure in place for your family that works for everyone. We've got to get a win-win. Otherwise, everyone loses. Let's go ahead and set up individual sessions."

"Fine with me," Tamara replied.

Reconstructing Chaos

Three days later, Tamara returned to Dr. Brightman's office. She was animated, but nervous, as she seated herself and began talking right away. "Doctor, I feel so relieved to know I don't have to discuss all of this in front of Kyle right now. He's been gone from home over a week, and I'm worried that the longer he stays away, the less likely he is to come back. I really have no one I can talk to about this, and of course I really can't discuss it with my mom. Mother has been so hurt by Kyle's behavior and I feel so sorry for her. He makes it obvious that he resents her, even though she's trying to help. Chelsea gives her so much joy, and Mother is totally devoted to her. It would break her heart not to have an important part in Chelsea's life. Dr. Brightman, I go to bed crying almost every night, because I can't see a way out of this. I feel so torn," she added, dabbing her eyes with a tissue.

"I understand Kyle's reasons for wanting things to change, but I can't bear to hurt my mom," Tamara continued. "Chelsea is doing so well now and I'm sure it's because of Mother. I couldn't have done it without her help."

"I know how much you want to protect your mother's feelings and would never want to hurt her. She has been a blessing for you," Dr. Brightman said reassuringly. Then she asked gingerly, "Have you thought any more about your mother seeing her doctor to determine if the new medicine is working?"

"I think it's working. She hasn't been coughing and wheezing lately. Actually, come to think of it, since Kyle left, she's been much better. But how am I going to tell her we don't need her as much as we did?"

"Don't mention leaving to her. Just remind her how helpful she has been. I want to ask you about something else now, Tamara. Do you think since your mother has taken over so many responsibilities involved in caring for Chelsea, that perhaps you have been left out of the learning curve?"

"Well, I know how dependent I've gotten on her for help. Truthfully, I'm nervous about taking on that role without her. What if I can't get Chelsea to stop crying? What if she chokes? I'm even afraid she might develop asthma, like Mother! You know, Chelsea was premature and had breathing problems after she was born. Sometimes when she's asleep, I wonder if she is still breathing. You know, we also had a rough couple of months after Chelsea was born. She had colic and cried a lot. Her formula didn't agree with her, and the pediatrician had us change it several times. I was frantic!" Tamara stopped to catch her breath.

"It sounds like you're not ready to completely let go of relying on your mother's help with Chelsea. So, we need to determine what you feel capable of doing and what you still feel anxious about. Are you still depressed, Tamara?"

"I'm much better now, but I'm still nervous about not having Mother there as a back-up."

"That's okay. But let's focus on those things that you're ready to change. For example, you cannot lose your relationship with your mother, but you can change her role in your life. You can't lose your relationship with Kyle, but you can change how you interact with him, and you both can learn parenting skills to help you feel more confident and competent. We need to start from here and make a plan. The challenge is having a loving relationship with your mother while still setting appropriate boundaries on her influence in your personal life and your family life."

"That'll take a miracle," Tamara stammered. "Frankly, it's overwhelming just thinking about it."

"I'm sure it is. Let's think about this for a moment. I don't believe you need to make the decision to return to work right now. First, I'd like to help you develop more confidence in being your child's primary caretaker. Why don't we make a plan? After your mother moves out, let's have her come over and coach you until you feel more secure in caring for Chelsea. We can focus on changing your mother's role from being a constant presence to that of a reliable resource when needed. How about trying that out a couple of days a week? Why not make a list of things that concern you, and ask for her suggestions? This should fulfill a necessary and important role for her in both your life and Chelsea's, and it won't seem like she's being pushed aside. I'm sure both of you can find some enjoyment in working as a team. You and your mother share the common goal of making Chelsea's well-being a top priority. This is a way we can negotiate a win-win situation. This will honor your mom's sense of purpose while bringing you more into the loop, as well as changing the way you relate to her."

"That's a lot. Sounds too good to be true. I just hope it will work," Tamara said with disbelief. "First, I've got to figure out how to ask Mother to leave without causing a scene."

"Maybe you can just tell her that you're getting too dependent on her and that you need to take more responsibility for Chelsea's care," the counselor suggested. "You can tell her you need her help and support with this. Here's an important point to consider, Tamara. I'm thinking she will need plenty of validation and appreciation for how well she's taught you and how grateful you are for her advice and experience. We need to make sure your mother comes away feeling appreciated for her efforts." "I love that idea! But how do you think Kyle will feel about me finding another excuse to keep my mother involved in our parenting?" Tamara inquired sheepishly.

"Well, that may take some consideration. You and Kyle also share the same basic goal regarding your daughter's welfare. If your mother can help you become more confident, Kyle should be pleased you don't need your mother as much. I'll discuss this with him in our private session; with your permission, of course.

"I'll definitely need your help with that, Dr. Brightman. I'm afraid to even mention Mother to Kyle at this point!" Tamara exclaimed. "He's still so angry and refuses to come home."

"I know you're worried, but we'll figure it out. How do you feel about what we've discussed?"

"I feel better now that we have a plan. I don't feel like I've been left hanging. I'll work on my concerns, make a list and have it ready for the next time we meet. I hope that I can pull this off with Mother, because I really miss Kyle and want him to come home. We still talk several times a day, and every night he complains about having to remain in the hotel for another night. He feels like Mother is holding him hostage there."

"I know you're both anxious about all of this, and I wish we could move it along faster. But let's get the plan in place and see what happens, okay?"

"Well, sounds like it's now or never!" Tamara responded.

"So, how about coming in the same time next week. Are you available?" Dr. Brightman looked over her appointment book.

Opening the Valve

A few days later, Kyle came to see Dr. Brightman. He appeared tentative and pensive as he entered the office and settled himself.

"Wow, Kyle, you look tired and stressed. What's going on?"

"This thing just seems to be dragging on and on, Doctor. When I first called you, I was wondering how and when we could get JoAnn out of our house, but the irony is that she's still there, and I'm the one that's out of our house! It couldn't be a more perfect scenario for JoAnn. At the end of every day after work, I can't look forward to seeing my wife and baby and eating a relaxing dinner. Instead, I typically pick up some fast food, flop onto the hotel bed with the TV remote, have a few drinks, watch some mindless programs and wonder how I got there. It's very lonely, Dr. Brightman. The highlight of my evening is calling Tamara. She says she misses me and is hurting over this, as well, but we're still stuck in this stalemate," he confessed bitterly. "I just want to be in my own home, in my own bed. This is really getting old."

"I'm sorry that leaving was the only way you could pull the plug on this escalating tension, Kyle. You've had to sacrifice a lot, but in Tamara's session this week, we outlined a plan that I'm going to share with you now. Tamara is in complete agreement that I discuss this with you. Basically, she has decided to delay going back to teaching. Instead, she has agreed that her first priority is learning to be confident in being a mom. Her depression, along with Chelsea's initial problems, caused a lot of anxiety and damaged Tamara's confidence in her role as a mother."

"You pegged it. It's like her mother hijacked Tamara's role."

"So, Tamara plans to ask JoAnn to leave, but come in during the day to support her until she can overcome her anxiety," Dr. Brightman finished.

"Hmmm…that sounds like JoAnn will still be in charge. And I doubt Tamara can hold her own against her mother."

"Kyle, we've got to take this in small steps, in order for it to work. In our sessions, I'm reinforcing Tamara's need to take more control over what she needs from JoAnn. It's my belief that when she feels better about herself, she won't be so anxious and need JoAnn's constant advice and reassurance. Tamara is coming back in the day after tomorrow, and I'm going to encourage her. We'll be role-playing how she is going to talk to JoAnn about this plan, so she won't be caught off-guard. We'll develop kind of a script in preparation for her encounter with JoAnn."

"Well, Tamara is going to need a lot of encouragement. She's pretty fragile," Kyle said, obviously unconvinced.

"It's very important for you to be patient and support Tamara's efforts in this plan. If she knows that she has your support, this will be much less stressful for her and you can soon move back home. From that point, we will begin to limit JoAnn's involvement, while we work on creating a better balance in Tamara's relationship with her. This needs to happen," Dr. Brightman paused. "So, you're on board with this idea, I hope? As long as we see progress, we will continue the plan. It's not an overnight fix, but I believe it will pay off."

"I've realized that it's not just the fact that JoAnn takes control of Chelsea that irks me," Kyle continued. "I'm much angrier that she continues to dictate everything Tamara does, and how she undermines me in Tamara's eyes. And Tamara's not strong enough to stop her. It really burns me up to see Tamara giving in to JoAnn time after time. She holds a more important place in Tamara's life than I do. What kind of marriage is that?"

"It's a triangle—not much of a marriage. But I think we can make a difference. Let's give this a chance to work and see how Tamara and JoAnn respond to the new arrangement, shall we?" Dr. Brightman encouraged.

Kyle nodded. He seemed to be absorbing the doctor's explanation. "Sure, Doctor. I suppose I have nothing to lose by holding on a little longer. But it's really not easy to keep my mouth shut when I'm talking to Tamara."

"It takes a lot of discipline, I know. Bite your tongue when you feel yourself beginning to boil. Take a 'timeout,' and stop the conversation. Talking when you're in emotional overload will only cause things to escalate."

"I'm on the boil all the time right now. But I get it. When I feel I'm going to say or do something I will regret later, I need to get some distance. That is why I moved out. If I had stayed, I know things would only have gotten worse," Kyle shook his head sadly.

"That tells me that I need to give you an assignment now, so listen carefully, please. You need a way to work through your feelings about this situation, so that you don't explode. My suggestion is to write a letter to JoAnn describing your frustration and anger and the impact that she has had on you and your marriage. I'm also giving you a Vocabulary List of Feelings (see page 197) so that you can label those feelings. You should understand that this letter is for therapeutic purposes only, to be read and shared only here, within our session. It is definitely not intended for sharing with JoAnn or Tamara. Just having the chance to express your feelings in writing should give you some release and help you collect your thoughts. Be absolutely open and honest with whatever you write. Bring the letter with you to your next session, and we will process it together."

"Now, we're talking!" Kyle exclaimed. "I might actually enjoy this homework assignment. I've been waiting for the right moment to really tell her off. I just wish I could say it to her face!" "This is a productive way for you to express your feelings without hurting anyone in the process and later regretting it," assured Dr. Brightman. "It sounds like you need this ASAP."

"Sure. When I have one of those explosions, I know it just pushes Tamara further away from me, and she always defends JoAnn."

"Right. There's no point in escalating the conflict. I'll help you work out the rest of the plan as we move forward. I'm going to give you a handout as a guideline to help you work on your letter this week. Bring it with you next time. Don't worry about how it comes out when you write it—it won't burst my ears! Just get it out. That's the main thing," Dr. Brightman urged, passing him the handout. "That's your homework assignment. Same time next week?" Dr. Brightman confirmed and walked with him toward the door.

A Mother's First Baby Steps

"Come on in, Tamara! Sit down and make yourself comfy. How's it going since last week?" Dr. Brightman queried.

"Well, Mother is still with us, and Kyle is still in the hotel, but he did tell me you went over our plan with him. Of course, nothing is going to work fast enough for him, but I think he's willing to give this a chance to play out."

"Before I comment on that, I need to let you know that Kyle has given me permission to discuss his sessions with you. I've talked with him about coming back home, Tamara, and he seems agreeable to our plan, but he's very impatient."

"Yeah, he says he feels like a trapped animal right now."

"Well, I'm sure he does feel trapped. It's like he's in a holding pattern. He doesn't want to stay there, but he doesn't feel like he can come home. Now, what about our plan? Did you get a chance to think about your list?"

"I did. I've listed several things."

"Have you mentioned any of this to your mother yet? Have you told her anything about our plan?"

"Every time I think about telling her, I panic. I'm afraid it will trigger one of Mother's asthma attacks. It's terrible to see her struggling to catch her breath and watching the color drain from her face as she gasps and chokes. I witnessed that so many times as a child. I had nightmares that she would die, and I would have no one—I'd be left alone! I would hate to be the cause of another one of those dreadful attacks," Tamara blinked back tears. "You know, Chelsea has had one respiratory infection after another since she was born. I've been so worried that she'll develop the same condition Mother has."

"I'm sure that was terrifying for you as a little girl, Tamara," Dr. Brightman responded. "But your mother does have her asthma under control now, doesn't she?"

"I think so, but I never know for sure. It's unpredictable."

"Did you ask your mother to write down some important suggestions for you?" the doctor inquired.

"I did and I posted them on the refrigerator. This first step seems to be working. She's always happy to comply when I need her. She sees how important she is."

"Good. Now, it's helpful to break the plan down into small chunks. How about trying some role-playing now? This will help you firm up your intentions, so that your mother doesn't throw you a curve."

"Good idea! How do we do that?"

"Let's create a scene, and I'll play your mother. Can you imagine yourself telling her about the plan? How do you feel about that?"

"Anxious. It's going to be hard for me. I want to be sure I don't sound ungrateful or mean," Tamara stammered.

"So, what do you want to say to her, Tamara? Pretend I'm her and tell me," Dr. Brightman prompted.

"Well, first, Mother—I want to tell you how much I appreciate you and how important it has been for me to have your help. After all we've been through, I couldn't have made it without you. But, sooner or later, I'm going to have to be a better mother to Chelsea than I am right now. I feel guilty that I have put so much on you, and you deserve a break. What I need from you now, Mother, is for you to support me in this."

"Hmph! It sounds like you're trying to give me my marching orders, Tamara! After all I've done for you, what is this all about? I'm sure Kyle put you up to this," Dr. Brightman parroted, assuming the role of JoAnn.

"Mother, you know I've been seeing this therapist, and she's helping me understand that I need to step up to the plate and take responsibility for myself and my daughter. She thinks it isn't fair that you've had to take such a long leave of absence from your work and sacrifice your time."

"So, what makes your therapist think this has been a sacrifice for me? I've enjoyed every minute of the time I've spent with Chelsea! And I want her to be just like you as she grows up—competing in pageants and modeling like you did. She's such a pretty baby, you know."

"She would say something exactly like that," Tamara spluttered. "And I don't have a comeback for that at all!"

"Well, maybe you could tell her that she's moving too fast for you, and that right now you want to be as good a mom to Chelsea as she has been to you," Dr. Brightman coached. "That's your goal, isn't it?"

"That's brilliant!" Tamara nodded.

Dr. Brightman went back into character and asked sarcastically, "You really think you can figure that out without me, Tamara?"

"I didn't say I wanted to do this without you, Mother. I said that I wanted us to do this together. I'm still going to need your help, but in a different way."

"Oh, really? How's that?" Dr. Brightman retorted, then shifting back to herself, she added, "This would be the point where you tell your mother about the plan."

"Mother, I want you to come over for a few hours during the day and I need to take care of things the rest of the time."

"I think you're biting off more than you can chew. You would probably panic," Dr. Brightman snapped, channeling Tamara's mother.

"I've read several books. And you've really helped me so much, Mother. Kyle has been reading some books, too, and he's promised to be there for me," Tamara replied, making her point.

"Kyle? What does he know about taking care of a baby—especially one who has had all the problems Chelsea's had."

"Chelsea isn't having those problems anymore. Thankfully, she has outgrown most of them," Tamara blurted. "Kyle needs to come home, and he won't, as long as you're here." Tamara set her jaw and looked sternly at Dr. Brightman.

"I think that therapist has brainwashed you. You're not yourself right now."

After a moment, Dr. Brightman went back to herself. "Okay, timeout. Keep playing this out in your mind, and I think you'll be able to stay on track when you talk to your mother. Your rehearsal went well. How do you feel?"

"It wasn't easy! I felt a knot in my stomach the whole time, but I just hope I can handle it without caving in to Mother," Tamara said, looking encouraged, but exhausted. "Once I get the message across, she'll love to supervise what I'm doing and of course, give plenty of advice. It's a natural role for her. Now, if I can just get her to leave without a big scene!"

"You did a great job today, and I'm proud of the way you're handling this. Next week okay for this same time?"

"Yes, please," Tamara said. "See you then!"

Tellin' it Like it Is

"Hey, Dr. Brightman! I've got an update for you," Kyle reported excitedly as he entered her office. "Tamara talked to her mother and I guess JoAnn got the message. She left in a huff yesterday and told Tamara to call her when she needed her. So, I took my cue from her exit, and I immediately checked out of the hotel and moved back home before she changes her mind. I think Tamara was shocked, but relieved. Maybe all this therapy is going to pay off, after all!"

"That's a huge leap forward, Kyle. I'm very proud of Tamara. You should know that she worked very hard to prepare herself for that encounter," Dr. Brightman informed him.

"I'm proud of her, too, and I tell her that over and over. I also told her that I will support her in working this out in every way I possibly can," Kyle smiled. "By the way, I've actually been looking forward to this session. I've brought my letter to JoAnn." Kyle pulled a folded sheet of paper from his pocket.

"Oh, good! I'm looking forward to hearing it."

Kyle settled comfortably on the couch.

"I'm glad I wrote this before I came back home, because I'm so happy to be back I might have been tempted to tone it down a bit. However, I still haven't forgotten how JoAnn nearly wrecked our family, and I'm concerned that she'll creep back in when Tamara's not expecting it. JoAnn knows Tamara's weaknesses and takes advantage of her. She just needs to get a life and stay out of ours," he snapped.

"Well, that will never happen. You know JoAnn is not going to leave Tamara and Chelsea out of her life. But I do believe she can learn to back off. Are you ready to read your letter?"

"You better believe it! It was pretty scathing at first, but I cleaned it up a little, so I don't think you'll be too offended. I really wanted to give it to her," Kyle warned, fuming. "Here goes!"

> *JoAnn:*
>
> *I'm enraged at your sense of entitlement. You think you have a right to control everything and anything in our lives! You make me sick with your constant interference and maneuverings! I can't stand the sight of you, but there's no way I could get away from you! You're always in our business, and we can't get rid of you! Rats and roaches would be easier to get rid of than you. I need a good pest-control service! You've monopolized Tamara's every*

move, and now you're targeting Chelsea! You've brainwashed Tamara to the point that she can't even make a simple decision anymore. All I hear from her is, "I don't know! Let me check with Mother!"

JoAnn, you destroyed your own marriage, and now you're determined to destroy mine! You've driven a huge wedge between Tamara and me, and you keep driving it in deeper and deeper. You're a vampire draining the life from our family! You are a toxic, controlling witch! I'm sick and tired of your manipulating Tamara with your phony asthma attacks. Any time she doesn't do exactly what you want, you guilt her into doing things your way. I'm warning you: I'm past the point of no return with your interference. I will no longer tolerate your constant interference!

Your sworn enemy,

Kyle

P. S. Take a long hike off a short pier—soon!

Kyle dropped the letter onto the couch and took a deep breath, trying to get a grip on himself. His reddened face reflected his deep-seated anger. "I actually wrote one that was much worse, but I'm going to keep that one locked up for a while. Hopefully, it won't spontaneously combust! It did help to spew out my anger, though. I just wish I could say those things to her face!" he exclaimed with a visible shudder.

"Of course, I would never recommend that," Dr. Brightman responded. "I think it was good for you to see your feelings on paper. If you hadn't gotten them out, you probably would have said or done something worse. You should probably continue to write about your anger. I'm sure there's still a lot in there. It's better than exploding."

"That would definitely keep me busy for a while. I haven't even begun to scratch the surface of how angry I feel."

"So, now that you have a better option than exploding, what's going on with you and Tamara?".

"I still resent the fact that Tamara continues to give JoAnn so much control over her life and never puts any limits on her, Dr. Brightman," Kyle blustered. "And I resent that she ignores my opinions and overrules my decisions constantly. I feel like I've been living in JoAnn's house—not my own!"

"So maybe you should write a letter to Tamara and get this out."

"What? That will be harder. I don't know. I love my wife, and I'm relieved to be back home, but I know there's still a lot of resentment under the surface," Kyle added, furrowing his brow.

"You know you can love someone and still be angry with them, right, Kyle? In fact, anger and love are usually closely linked."

"I'll see how it goes. See you next week," Kyle said soberly, as he exited clumsily out the door.

Drawing a Line in the Sand

Tamara's shoulders ached with tension as she shifted about in search of a more comfortable position on the sofa. She had a lot on her mind and was anxious to talk with Dr. Brightman about it all.

"Hi, Tamara, what's going on? You look a stressed. Are you feeling alright?" Dr. Brightman asked with concern, passing her a bottle of cold water.

"Just a little tense, I suppose. A lot has happened since we last met," Tamara sighed, running her fingers through the short waves of her caramel-colored hair.

"What's going on?" Dr. Brightman asked with concern.

"Well, first, I know Kyle came in the other day to see you and told you that he's back home now. That was a big step. We're looking forward to becoming the family we've always wanted to be. And, yes, Dr.

Brightman—I did it! I had that talk with Mother, and it played out a lot like we role-played in our session. That exercise really helped me. I kept it in mind the whole time I was talking to her, and I felt a lot steadier when she protested.

I took your advice and thanked Mother for her help, but when I told her that I wasn't going to need her help as much, she balked. Just as we predicted, she tried to make me feel guilty and commented that she feared I might have some difficulty that I couldn't handle. 'What are you going to do then,' she demanded. When I didn't back down, she seemed shocked and asked, 'So, does this mean you're not going to need me to stay here anymore?' You know, I can't slide anything past her!"

Dr. Brightman consoled her. "That took a lot of courage for you to put that out there for your mother. You must have been pretty anxious."

"Actually, I did better than I thought I would, but my voice trembled the entire time I was talking with her. I'm not used to telling Mother what I want her to do. She's usually the one telling *me* what to do. It felt very awkward, like I was doing something wrong. It seemed like I was disrespecting her and being mean, because I knew it would hurt her. I hated seeing that stunned look on her face, Doctor. But somehow I found the strength to say 'Mother, I've got to be able to do this!'"

"That's a typical reaction. When you set boundaries, people try to pull you back into that old pattern, so it makes it hard to stick to your point. You need to know that it's normal to get resistance when you're trying to set a healthy boundary around yourself. People don't like it. You should be prepared for a backlash," Dr. Brightman cautioned.

"You mean there's another asthma attack coming? That's kind of scary! I told you what it was like for me to see those life-threatening asthma attacks when I was a child. So, I guess it's a trigger for me when Chelsea has a cough or congestion. At the moment, it feels life-threatening. Anyway, I know that's probably irrational, but my anxiety goes through the roof," Tamara confessed.

"I'm sure that was terrifying for you, and you felt so helpless when you were a child. But remember that your mother survived those attacks, and there are much better methods for treating that problem now. You know, you can always call 911 if there's an emergency," Dr. Brightman reassured her.

"I know you're right; I have better options now. Thanks for the warning that Mother could strike again with another 'asthma attack.'" Tamara made air quotes with her fingers. "I'll be on the alert in case she tries something. Doctor, before Kyle convinced me to come see you, I complained to him that you couldn't possibly help us, since you don't even know Mother. Now, I believe you know her all too well! Mother certainly knows exactly how to push my buttons and make me feel guilty."

"It is hard to set boundaries with your mother, and it's even harder to maintain them. There may be times when you feel like giving in, Tamara, but then you lose ground and have to start over. You can expect her to try to manipulate you, one way or another; that's her pattern. You will have to be on alert so you won't get dragged into whatever manipulations she comes up with."

"Well, I hadn't even brought up the subject of asking Mother to leave, but she immediately jumped to that conclusion. She got very indignant, and curtly told me, 'Tamara, I think you're getting in over your head. I don't think you're ready for this!'"

(Note: A mother speaking insecurity and anxiety into her daughter is a setup for failure so that she will be able to reestablish the old dysfunctional pattern. That is typical when a boundary is established.)

"She's using all the old tactics. What happened then?" Dr. Brightman inquired curiously.

"Well, then Mother immediately marched into the guest bedroom and started grabbing up her things. I followed her into the room and told her, 'Nobody said you have to leave right this minute.' But she took her things and left, saying, 'I know when I'm not wanted.'" Tamara rubbed her head nervously. "I can't say that didn't make me anxious, Doctor. But it feels good knowing that I didn't back down."

"Tamara, believe me. You're stronger than you think," the counselor reassured her. "You have come a long way."

"I hope so. I called Mother the next morning and asked her to come over to the house to go over a list I'd made. I took your advice and really appealed to her compulsion to feel needed. At first, she sounded put out with me, but finally she agreed to come over later. It seems to be an uneasy truce, but so far, so good."

"You're doing all the right things. Let's explore another idea now. Perhaps you could suggest to your mother that she resume her marketing responsibilities at the department store, or any other interests she might like to pursue."

"Well, she's never been too involved in outside activities. Her work in the marketing department of the store has been her main focus, except for me. She's always bringing home new outfits for me and now for Chelsea. I'll see if I can strike up a conversation and see where it goes. Besides, now that I've gotten back into shape after having the baby, I'd like to look for a new wardrobe. Mother has a sharp eye for fashion, and she'd probably love to pick out some outfits for me to try on."

"Great! That will do a lot to change her focus," Dr. Brightman speculated.

"Well, okay—I guess we'll see what happens next, Tamara said thoughtfully. "Kyle couldn't wait to come home, but I know he's still resentful toward me. Otherwise, he seems happy and relieved and is enjoying 'Daddy-time' with Chelsea. I'll see you next week with an update."

The Ugly Truth

Kyle's mood was brooding as he lumbered slowly into the office. Dr. Brightman could almost hear his bones creaking beneath the burden in his heart as he sank his six-foot frame into the deep cushions of a chair. "Doc," Kyle said wearily, "I'm so glad to be home again. But, truthfully, things are still pretty tense around there." He offered a forced smile. "Tamara and her mother have had, shall we say, some rather unpleasant and lively conversations. They've pretty much drained Tamara, but she mostly held her ground and was able to, as you would say, 'negotiate more reasonable boundaries' with JoAnn. That's a real step forward."

"My goodness, that is a really big step forward!" Dr. Brightman exclaimed. "What impact are these changes having on you?" she asked as she handed him a bottle of water.

"Thanks. I guess you could say that I'm having mixed feelings about it. Looking back, I can see that we've made progress, and I'm both surprised and hopeful. But, I still feel a lot of uncertainty. You know, I'm proud of Tamara for her effort in setting some new boundaries with JoAnn, but she has such a strong influence, that I wonder if Tamara will be able to maintain those boundaries. I'm still afraid that she's going to give in if her mother pressures her too much or has another 'asthma attack,'" Kyle used air quotes.

"That's a fair assessment. And you're right: setting boundaries is often easier than keeping them. It seems that those with a habit of violating boundaries will usually find another way to gain an advantage," the doctor cautioned.

"I guess I'm already on the lookout for JoAnn's next maneuver to try to lure Tamara back into the old pattern," he confessed.

"Good for you, Kyle! You should be aware of that probability. You're going to have to be on the alert for a while. But remember, it's Tamara's responsibility to keep the boundaries she's set with JoAnn. Not yours."

"Well, she's setting boundaries with me too. Even though her mother is gone, she is distant and still blames me for throwing JoAnn under the bus. She sees me as the 'Boogey Man,'" Kyle griped.

"It may take a while before Tamara can actually face the damage her mother has caused, Kyle. But what about that letter to Tamara we talked about last week? Were you able to get in touch with your resentment?"

"I was kind of hoping you'd forget about that. I'm just a little worked up about reading it today, though." Kyle paused to twist the lid off the water bottle.

"Oh, so you were able to write that letter to Tamara? Was it harder to do than you thought it would be?"

"Well, I have to say that the effect of writing Tamara's letter was entirely different for me than when I wrote to JoAnn. Writing about anger to JoAnn felt cathartic, almost energizing and empowering. It felt really good to get those feelings out and be able to say what I always wanted to say but couldn't!" Kyle related, his eyes shining. "The letter to JoAnn just poured out of me all at once. But it was really hard to get through this one. It came out in short spurts. I'd get started, but then I'd get sort of overwhelmed and have to walk away from it for a while. I have so many mixed emotions. I actually felt a little guilty when I was writing it, because I know Tamara's doing the best she can. I feel like I'm doing something wrong, cutting loose on her with this letter."

"Yes, I thought this letter might be harder for you than the one you wrote to JoAnn. If you're ready, go ahead and read it now."

"Right—let's get on with it." He retrieved the folded page from his breast pocket.

Tamara, Dearest—

I'm so sick and tired of living like a stranger in my own home, constantly overruled and discounted by your controlling Rottweiler of a mother! You have no idea what this has done to me, and you don't even seem to care. All you care about is appeasing the Rottweiler! If she is the most important person in your life, maybe you should just go back to her. You don't seem to need me

anyway. I'm just in the way, aren't I? But I'm telling you this
right now: I'm not gonna stand by and turn the other cheek any
longer. I'm going to stand up to her whether you do or not! I've
been pushed past my limit. So, you're going to have to make a
choice: it's your mother or me. When are you going to grow up
and act like my wife, instead of a pitiful child? I hope you get the
picture. You'd better find a way to rid us of this nuisance ASAP! I
can't go on like this.

　　Resentfully,
　　Kyle

Kyle looked agitated as he refolded the letter, putting it back into his breast pocket. Then he began to sob from the pain he had held in for years. Dr. Brightman sat silently, allowing him to release his emotions. After catching his breath, he spoke again.

"That sounded like a threat, didn't it? What's happened to us? How could things have gotten so far off track? I'm saying things I never thought I would ever say," Kyle seethed, "but there's no way I can live like this any longer!"

"I can see that you've mined through several layers of emotions. I know that letter was very difficult to finish. It's obvious it touched on some deep-seated pain. Can you put words to it?" Dr. Brightman urged.

"Grief, anger, disappointment, regret—things that I now realize I've lived with for years. Tamara never even seemed to notice how difficult JoAnn made things for us—especially me," Kyle sighed. "I guess writing this made it pretty clear that I've held in a lot of bitterness for a very long time. That's why I explode. I knew how much I resented JoAnn, but writing this letter really helped me realize that I'm resentful toward Tamara as well. I thought Tamara should have stopped this whole thing a long time ago, but she's allowed it to continue. She's been as much a part of this as JoAnn. She's been the weak link. I wonder if I can ever trust her to keep JoAnn in line," Kyle mused indignantly. "It made me realize that no marriage could endure this. We really were at the end of our rope, weren't we?"

"If that pattern had continued, I couldn't see much of a chance for your marriage."

"Well, for what it's worth, writing that letter helped clear my mind and has given me the courage to set my own boundaries and never let things go back there again."

"What do you mean?"

"I'm going to be very clear with Tamara about what I will and will not tolerate regarding 'JoAnn boundaries' if we're going to have any peace. It's my house, too, after all, and I should be Tamara's first priority, not JoAnn," Kyle stated somberly.

"When Tamara sets boundaries with JoAnn, you will have to support these boundaries, as well, Kyle, and remind her when she waivers. I've warned Tamara about the danger of the backlash she's likely to get from JoAnn. She will most certainly attempt to draw Tamara back into her ways of doing things and manipulate her with guilt. Just for the record, I'm reminding you to be prepared for JoAnn's schemes," Dr. Brightman warned.

"Believe me, I won't have any trouble giving Tamara all the support she needs—and with relish! I just hope she will accept it. This is the very thing I've been waiting forever for her to do. But, thanks for the warning! I'll be watching for one of those phony asthma attacks," Kyle huffed snidely.

"That's JoAnn's M.O., so you're wise to be on your guard. Thank you for writing that letter. I know it was hard, but maybe now you can get it out of your head for a while and go home and relax. See you next week," Dr. Brightman said warmly as she walked Kyle out the door.

Creating an Inspired Legacy

"Welcome back, Tamara. I'm eager to hear how the changing of the guards went!" Dr. Brightman smiled as Tamara settled in. "Did it go as smoothly as we planned?"

"Well, the inevitable happened, just as you warned me. Mother was supposed to come over at eight thirty the morning after she left. About seven o'clock, I got a call, however. She was wheezing and coughing but managed to ask me how everything had gone overnight. I told her I felt like everything had gone pretty well, with no unexpected problems, but I guess that was the wrong thing to say. Mother's wheezing got even louder, and then she said, 'I hope this spell doesn't turn into pneumonia like has happened before. I coughed all night long and didn't get a wink of sleep. I had to use my nebulizer several times, and it's not working as well as it usually does.' So, I asked Mother if she had called the doctor, but she just said she wanted to wait to see if things might settle down on their own. She was trying to scare me, Dr. Brightman. Miraculously, she soon revived and arrived by noon. Of course, she grabbed Chelsea out of my arms as soon as she came through the door. Mother then informed me the baby was outgrowing her clothes and needed a new wardrobe. She said she would pick out several outfits from the store and bring them over later this week. Then, guess what I heard? 'We've got to start getting Chelsea ready for the pageants!' She also mentioned that she had scheduled a photographer to come over to photograph Chelsea in her outfits. My head was spinning, but fortunately, she managed to sneak out the door just before Kyle came home from work. So, is that progress? I'm not sure what to think," Tamara added doubtfully.

"Wow, she's still working every angle, isn't she?" Dr. Brightman exclaimed. "It sounds like she's already maneuvering her position."

"Yeah, but guess what? I've come up with an idea that might help with Mother, and I'd like to share it with you."

"Tell me about it."

"Well, now that she is about to return to her management position in fashion marketing, I remembered how happy she was when I was a child and modeled the clothes she picked out for me. I was just a toddler when I started, and there are probably hundreds of photographs of me participating in those fashion shoots. Of course, Chelsea is just a baby, but Mother's department puts out a catalog every season, and it always features pictures of babies and toddlers in adorable outfits. I'm thinking about mentioning to Mother that I would like to have Chelsea featured in the store's infant wear section of the catalog. I hate to admit it, but I must have inherited some of those fashion genes from Mother, and I'd be excited to see Chelsea appear in those catalogs ! I think Mother will be ecstatic over this idea. She could pick out the clothes and dress Chelsea and get her ready for the photographer. Of course, I'd be there, too, but Mother would be in charge, and since she works at Mon Chez Moi, she would have no trouble arranging all the details. Mother would feel important, and be involved, but in a different way, and we'd have something fun to share. What do you think?"

"I think that's a great suggestion for a new direction!" Dr. Brightman affirmed.

"That's my cue then, Doctor," Tamara said proudly, showing her some photos on her cell phone. "Look at these! Mother brings Chelsea the most adorable clothes along with a new toy or stuffed animal every time she comes over. She's doing her best to spoil her already," Tamara accused, her look of adoration fading to concern.

"Aww…she is adorable! And I think this idea is perfect and will keep your mother involved in Chelsea's life. Something that's right up her alley! It will bring back positive memories for both your mother and you. When you ask her about this, you could tell her that this might just start a family legacy!" Dr. Brightman laughed. "I don't know if you realize it, but you've really come a long way in the last several sessions. That's very considerate of you to want to include your mother in a new role by offering her something with her granddaughter that she will enjoy so much. I think she'll be eager to start working on this right away. This idea looks like it can be a real win-win, for you, Chelsea, your mother, and of course, Kyle, when your Mother's energy is redirected. Fantastic move!"

"Thanks," Tamara smiled. "I'm glad you think so."

"And, you brought up another point. Will you be able to let your mother know she needs to limit the toys and gifts in the future? She's out of bounds here already. These are boundary issues, as well."

Tamera wondered, "How can I say that without hurting her feelings?" "Just say something like, 'Mother, you're the most generous person I know, but maybe too generous. We don't want to spoil Chelsea and have her expect you to bring her something every time she sees you.' What do you think about that?"

"I like that; it compliments, but also limits her. It's like that Mary Poppins song, 'A spoonful of sugar helps the medicine go down...' I actually feel kind of inspired. I really don't remember another time I was able to do something nice for Mother that didn't feel like it was taking something away from me!"

"Now, you're really onto something! I want you to remember that feeling. Feeling like you're doing something for someone that doesn't compromise your own well-being and needs. That's the barometer for determining a healthy boundary," Dr. Brightman emphasized.

"This feeling is empowering and positive—And I don't feel guilty!"

"No need to feel guilty. You should feel proud of yourself," Dr. Brightman confirmed. "Hope you have a wonderful week, Tamara."

"You know, I'm beginning to feel like I *can* have a wonderful week, Dr. Brightman, thanks to your help. And I hope your week is wonderful, as well," Tamara squeezed the doctor's hand as she rose to leave.

Chambers Unlocked

Dr. Brightman almost didn't recognize the Chambers when they both entered her office. Their facial expressions and body language seemed transformed from their past sessions. They seemed more relaxed and engaged with one another. The counselor immediately liked what she saw.

"Come in, you two," the doctor greeted. "It's good to see you again. Let's take some time to have you both tell me where you think things stand. You've done a lot of hard work, and I know it hasn't been easy. Well, who wants to start?"

"I'll go first, if that's okay," Kyle offered, revealing a newly rediscovered grin. "I never believed we'd get this far when we started this journey with you. It seemed like an impossible situation."

"What's changed, Kyle? What's different now?"

"A lot of changes have taken place, Doctor. It's still challenging for Tamara, but she's doing a great job of keeping her boundaries with JoAnn, so that makes me less resentful and angry. I'm not ready to snap her head off at the slightest provocation any longer. I'm really enjoying my daughter now, but I'm still wondering if this is all a dream—if it will last. Of course, I would rather not have JoAnn involved in our family at all, but at least she doesn't completely dominate us anymore. So, we're starting to look like a real family!"

"That's music to my ears, Kyle. I know it took a lot of restraint and patience on your part to get to this point, particularly in the beginning. I know how much this disturbed you. I'm glad you stuck it out and gave it a chance to work. And I get it: you can be respectful to JoAnn and still keep your distance. It doesn't mean you have to like her."

"Thank you for that, Dr. Brightman! I definitely want to keep my distance, and I think I can manage to be polite at least for short periods of time. It helps that Tamara and I are getting reconnected, so I feel more like making the effort," Kyle replied.

"What about you, Tamara?" Dr. Brightman questioned.

"I know you remember how concerned I was about hurting Mother when we started out," Tamara began. "I feel like we really dodged a bullet here! I don't think Mother cares for the limits we've set, but I did approach her about my catalog idea, and she immediately latched onto it. She's already planned the whole layout and contacted a well-known photographer! This has given her a new role in Chelsea's life. Setting this up will occupy a lot of her time and energy. Truth be told, she'll probably enjoy this much more than diaper changes and midnight feedings. She still likes to give me directions about Chelsea's needs and care; I should do this, or I shouldn't do that, but it doesn't bother me nearly as much as it used to. I try to take it with a grain of salt. I still catch myself feeling guilty sometimes, though, as if I think I could have handled some things better."

"Yes, but you're rebounding a lot better than I thought you would," Kyle interjected. "You actually seem to enjoy Chelsea, now that the Rottweiler isn't snarling around us all the time. I know JoAnn continues to try to put a guilt trip on you, but I see you pressing through it."

"Thank you for that, Kyle. It's so good to hear you say that!" Tamara responded.

"Everyone makes mistakes sometimes, Tamara," Dr. Brightman reassured, "so try not to put unrealistic expectations on yourself. You don't have to be perfect—no one is. If you set your expectations too high, you'll feel like a failure when you can't meet them. You and Kyle are doing a good job of balancing your relationship with JoAnn. Now you can see what I meant when I said boundaries eliminate a lot of chaos in our lives," she noted.

"I realize looking back, that I was depressed and emotionally unprepared to handle my daughter's needs on my own. It was hard to see myself in such a downward spiral," Tamara admitted.

"No one likes to feel helpless, Tamara. I want you to know that I'm very pleased with your progress, and you've proven your ability to follow through."

"More like 'crawl' through!" Tamara joked.

"Let me run through some of the progress you've made with your boundaries. As you formed your identity as a unified couple, you were able to set necessary boundaries to reestablish the integrity of your marriage," the doctor outlined. "Remember, boundaries are about negotiating closeness and distance. You needed to create *distance* with JoAnn, who was destabilizing your marriage, and then reestablish *closeness* with each other. Now, you need to be aware of the effect others have on you and set the appropriate boundaries when they are intrusive. Then your relationships will come into proper balance. Remember, if you don't manage your own lives, someone or something else will. Any thoughts on this?"

"Amazing principle, Dr. Brightman!" Kyle chuckled. "If we had known this earlier, we wouldn't have come so close to a divorce."

"I wish this were as easy to do as it sounds, but thanks to your guidance and direction, it changed our marriage," Tamara chimed in. "I'm glad we have those handouts. I'm sure we're going to need them going forward."

"I have to congratulate you both for your work on negotiating some very tricky boundaries. As for now, you seem to be in a good place, so I think the main goal of our therapy has basically been accomplished. I'm going to suggest you come back in a month for a checkup. Of course, you can call me in the meantime if a problem arises. I think you're on the way to creating the life you told me you wanted when you first came in. Just keep doing what you're doing, and you'll keep getting what you're getting," Dr. Brightman quipped, as she ended their session. "Now for a request: Would you please send me a link to that catalog with Chelsea's pictures in it when it comes out?"

"We'd love to, Dr. Brightman!" Tamara grinned.

Kyle reiterated, "As if you had a choice, Doctor. We've already added your name to the mailing list!" "And so it goes," Dr. Brightman replied. "We could say that your stumbling blocks have become stepping-stones.

• • •

Postpartum Depression

What is postpartum depression? It is a type of depression that many women experience after the birth of their baby due to hormonal changes. Its onset commonly begins within 2 to 3 days after giving birth, and may last for months.

About 15% of pregnant women suffer from depression following childbirth.

New mothers experiencing postpartum depression feel sadness, anxiety, hopelessness, or despair, as well as feelings of guilt and irritability.

They reported behaviors that were unusual for them:

- Crying a lot, sometimes for no reason
- Feeling unable to care for their babies
- Trouble feeling bonded to their babies
- A loss of interest in food, self-care or other activities they once enjoyed
- Sleeping too much
- An inability to focus, learn or remember.

Many responded positively to diverse forms of treatment, including:

- Doctor-prescribed antidepressants
- Professional counseling helped where patients were encouraged to process feelings, as well as learn coping skills to challenge negative thoughts

- Attention to self-care and exercise
- Participation in activities that previously made them happy
- An intact support system
- Lessening responsibilities so they did not feel so overwhelmed
- Surrounding themselves with caring people who are willing to help.

Emergency: Any woman having obsessive and fearful thoughts about harming herself or her baby MUST seek immediate emergency medical attention.

P.S. Did you notice how, in this situation, appropriate boundaries allowed Tamara and Kyle to reestablish their marriage and also allowed JoAnn to engage with her granddaughter in a meaningful way? This is an example of negotiating a win-win solution in an emotionally complicated personal boundary situation.

The Sloans

CHAPTER 2

The Interloper

Many couples have experienced the devastating impact of an extramarital affair. This creates an emotional earthquake that shatters the fabric of the marriage and turns their world upside down. Read on as Sharon and Stephen Sloan go on a step-by-step journey to get their bearings. See how they process feelings of betrayal, anger, and hurt and learn specific skills to re-establish their marriage.

P.S. Sharon and Stephen represent couples who desire to put the past behind them and restore their marriage. Unfortunately, there are others who do not wish to continue the marriage and opt for divorce, bypassing the therapeutic process.

Warning!

For anyone who has ever experienced an affair or been the "other" party in an affair, this case study may bring back painful or unsettling memories.

Marital Outsourcing

Stephen miserably paced the reception area of the marriage counselor's office. Despite the room's comforting amber tone, he was definitely not looking forward to this encounter. He wiped his sweaty palms on the front of his stylish printed shirt and sat down in an overstuffed tapestry-covered chair beneath the double windows across the room from his wife, Sharon. He impatiently plucked a piece of lint from the crease of his khaki slacks, interlocked his fingers and leaned forward in the chair with his forearms on his knees. He hated feeling at the mercy of a process that he had no guarantee would benefit his floundering marriage of fourteen years. For crying out loud! He was a forty-four year old airline pilot who'd successfully transported thousands of people safely to their destinations and the father of three active boys. How could he be feeling like a helpless, guilty child at the prospect of this journey?

Why can't this just be over? Stephen wondered to himself. He was so sorry he'd hurt Sharon by having the affair with Holly. He'd told Sharon this a million times. But she just couldn't seem to get past it. The hurt, the sense of betrayal, the feeling that she just wasn't enough for him anymore—he saw it clearly painted across Sharon's perfectly made-up face every time he looked at her. He felt responsible for her pain, and that was why he'd agreed to come here. He supposed he deserved to feel as wretched as he did. He squeezed his usually twinkly baby-blue eyes shut and ran his hands through his salt-and-pepper hair, silently praying for a way through this.

When he was honest with himself, however, Stephen had to admit that though he regretted hurting Sharon and was really sorry he'd had the affair, he still had lingering feelings for Holly. Although he'd ended things with her after Sharon had discovered their sexy texts on his cell phone, he was still struggling with the desire to reconnect. And Holly, a force to be reckoned with, was still pursuing Stephen.

Stephen felt that Sharon's attentions had long been diverted from him to her successful interior design business. She had a sense of style, whether it was her own or helping clients find a way to express their personal tastes through decor. Stephen actually appreciated that about Sharon. She could create an aura in an empty room the way he commandeered the airspace from the cockpit of a Boeing 777. His schedule required that he be away from her frequently, and he'd never understood why she couldn't carve out more time for him while he was home.

The boys were actively involved with baseball and soccer games, and weekends always revolved around their games. The family spent a lot of time driving back and forth between various ballparks and playing fields in the suburbs near their upscale home. This was both a blessing and a curse, as far as Stephen was concerned. At least they all remained too busy to notice the tensions that lingered in the air, and he enjoyed being able to lose himself temporarily in the excitement of the boys' games.

Stephen eventually started "doing some online research" on his computer in their study and sleeping on the hobnailed leather sofa there. That's where he received Holly's late-night text messages and began communicating with her regularly. He was careful to delete the trail of messages from his PC but forgot to be as stringent with the few the pair had managed by cell phone.

Stephen recalled the day Sharon discovered their affair. On a suspicion, she had picked up his phone from the kitchen counter one morning. While he was outside repairing a broken sprinkler system, Sharon downloaded the phone's history, and got a clear picture of the shocking extent of his involvement with Holly.

He came back inside to find Sharon screaming and crying. She shoved the phone in his face, pointing to a sexy photo Holly had texted him. Ugh! He should have deleted that, but he liked the picture. He tried to dismiss the photo as a joke that held no significance and was relieved when it seemed Sharon had dropped the matter. From now on, he'd be more careful, he told himself.

And now, here they were. It seemed they'd been sitting in the reception area for hours, but in fact, it had been less than ten minutes. As he sat waiting to see the counselor, Stephen's burden increased with the thought of maybe having to discuss his affair with Holly, and the difficulty of admitting that he still had feelings for her. He wasn't ready to completely let go.

He realized for the first time that even if he and Sharon failed to save their marriage, he was going to have to find a way to cooperate with her in order to co-parent their sons. No matter what happened, Sharon was going to be a part of his life forever as the mother of their children. Future milestones like graduations, marriages, holidays, and grandchildren had to be factored into their relationship. He was so conflicted with all his opposing emotions, mind swirled with all these scenarios as he stretched his aching neck and sighed.

1 + 1 = 3

Sharon's neck and shoulders also ached with the tension that now seemed to be her constant companion. She shifted uncomfortably on the overstuffed couch and wrapped one hand around the back of her neck, trying to release some of the knots that resided there. Finally, she surrendered to the habitual necessity of rummaging through her designer bag for her water bottle and anti-anxiety medication. Exposing the deeply painful mess of her private life to this marriage counselor wasn't going to be easy, but part of her looked forward to releasing the thoughts and emotions she'd been bottling up.

Sharon was regarded by her friends and clients as a casually elegant woman, dignified and graced with classic beauty. She was rarely trendy in her dress, preferring to buy a few really nice wardrobe pieces every year, and updating her accessories seasonally. In the last few weeks, however, she seemed to be in a rut of wearing beiges and black and white outfits, as if all the color in her heart had bled out along with her tears. She wore her highlighted hair long, changing the style regularly to suit her mood or her outfit.

Sharon had insisted that she and Stephen keep the truth of his affair from their sons. Until the two of them decided what they were going to do about their marriage, she saw no point in dragging the boys through this muck. Let them enjoy their innocence while they could. But they were clever, sensitive young boys, and Sharon sensed they had figured out that things were not going smoothly between their parents. It was a strain to keep up appearances for their sake, hiding her tears while dodging their questions and quizzical expressions.

Sharon had never expected anything like this from Stephen. It had turned her world inside out. She knew when she started her interior design business, that they would both have to make sacrifices. She had taken great care to explain to Stephen how much building this business meant to her. Fair was fair, after all. She certainly understood how much commercial flying meant to him. And she felt that she was more than accommodating, juggling her clients as well as she could, and managing the care of the boys. When did all this get so out of hand? Had their career passions and the challenges of raising three children slowly distanced them from one another? Or had they turned to their careers and parenting activities to avoid noticing their ebbing affections?

The flood of emotions Sharon felt only made her head and neck throb more intensely. Life would never again be the same for her. These were thoughts and emotions she was unfamiliar with. Shock, loss, betrayal, and anger were obvious reactions to the discovery of Stephen's affair. But she also felt failure, as if somehow she'd been judged as "not enough." Most baffling of all, she felt some guilt. *Was she really better than I am? Why wasn't I enough for him? What's wrong with me that he would do this?* But then again, why in heaven's name should she feel guilty? She wasn't the one who had broken their vows, after all. Lately, however, she'd been questioning herself. If Stephen had been so unhappy with her, why hadn't he told her? They could have sought counseling at that point, before all this had happened. If only she'd known.

Sharon took a swig of water, and then traded the bottle for a lipstick tube in her purse. As she reapplied her lip stain, the doctor called for her and Stephen to enter the counselor's office.

Dr. Carla Brightman smiled broadly as she crossed the Persian rug that graced the floor and welcomed the Sloans into her office. The tension between them was tangible, and she could see that her first order of business was going to be getting them to relax a little.

"Would you like some water or coffee to drink?" she offered.

Stephen opted for coffee, and Sharon retrieved her water bottle from her purse, as they settled onto opposite ends of the plush couch.

"So, tell me what's going on," Dr. Brightman began. "Sharon, when you told me over the phone that Stephen had had an affair, you said that you were both very confused and overwhelmed, and needed to figure out what to do next. That's when we agreed to set this appointment to explore your options." Noticing their tension and discomfort, she continued, "You need to fill me in on what's happened up to this point. So, who wants to start?" The doctor wasn't surprised to see Sharon take the lead in sharing her story.

"Well, to be frank, I don't feel I have a marriage any longer. I feel like the breath has been knocked out of me—like I'm living in a surreal world," Sharon quipped, her face suddenly reddening as she turned to look at her husband.

"This is definitely overwhelming, Sharon. It's turned your whole world upside down, hasn't it?" Dr. Brightman asked. Sharon nodded tensely. "When did you first discover that something was wrong?"

"Well, let's see. I took on a major decorating project with a short deadline. Most nights I fell asleep thumbing through my sample books, trying to get ideas. Of course, having my books all over the bed irritated Stephen, and he'd complain that he couldn't sleep comfortably in his own bed. So, his excuse was to sleep on the leather couch in the study, 'to get some decent rest.' The irony was that there was nothing 'decent' about it! Even after I moved my books off the bed and apologized, he insisted that he didn't want to be a bother and remained in the study at night, continuing to sleep on the couch. I was a little suspicious at this point, but brushed it off because it was so out of character for him.

"In my wildest dreams, I had no idea that he was in there sending messages back and forth with this bimbo flight attendant!" she stammered, choking on her words. "I know he tried to cover his tracks, because a couple of times he shut down his computer very quickly when I came downstairs to see if he was coming to bed. One morning, I had a random thought to pick up his phone while he was outside. You can imagine my shock, when I opened a text from a woman and found a risqué photo with a provocative message addressed to Stephen! When he came in and saw me staring at his phone, he looked horrified. I shoved the picture on the screen into his face and demanded to know what was going on. It was ridiculous for him to try to deny the obvious truth. But he did, saying that this text was just random chatter and that the girl meant nothing to him. I think he actually thought I believed him. Sorry, Stephen. You're just not that convincing of a liar, and you certainly can't 'delete' the memory of what I saw with my own eyes!"

Stephen was clearly in a panic, looking to Dr. Brightman for some kind of intervention on his behalf. He looked like a trapped animal, desperate to escape.

"I am just ready to explode," Sharon ranted. "Stephen, you've wrecked everything we had!" She began shaking as tears flooded her face. "I really hate you for this! How could you do this to me? How could you do it to the boys? You've torn my heart in two, and I'll never trust you again!"

Dr. Brightman turned to her, "I'm so sorry, Sharon. No wonder you're so devastated. This is the ultimate betrayal to a marriage."

"That's exactly right. That's a good way to put it. I am shattered. Everything I thought was real... isn't," Sharon said sadly.

"What are you hearing, Stephen?" the counselor asked.

"Well, it's obvious that I screwed up. I'm the one who caused this pain, and I don't like seeing Sharon like this," he blurted. "I guess I thought I could get away with it, and that she would never know. I certainly didn't intend to hurt her. I've told her dozens of times how sorry I am. I made a mistake. It was wrong, but I really don't know what else I can do," his voice trailed off.

"Well, there's plenty that we can do," the doctor responded. "I want to give you both some hope and encouragement today."

"I've told you over and over again how sorry I am, Sharon," Stephen continued. "I get that I was wrong, but you just won't let this go! Why can't we just put this entire thing behind us? I've cut it off with Holly, and I'm not seeing her anymore. I've tried everything I can think of to make it up to you. I even bought you that gold and diamond bracelet you wanted. But you call it a 'guilt trinket' and refuse to wear it! You constantly remind me of what I've done and question me again and again about every detail. You just won't get off my back. What more do you want from me? I honestly don't know what more I can do!" he implored, looking dejectedly at Sharon.

Stephen's whole demeanor suddenly shifted. He dropped his head into his hands and stared at the floor, trying to distract himself from the emotion he felt.

"Stephen, I know this is tough, but you need to get these feelings out," Dr. Brightman urged. "Please, can you continue?"

"I feel so much guilt and shame. I never thought I could get caught up in something like this. I'm usually the one in control, and losing it like this makes me feel so stupid and weak. It really hurts knowing that my actions are the reason for Sharon's misery and my own," he admitted, with a groan.

"It's good that you are being so open. Acknowledging your responsibility and recognizing the impact this has had on you both will be crucial steps in the recovery process. We could use the analogy of a broken leg. You can ignore the pain and suffering it causes and continue to try walking on it, but then it will never heal properly. You would probably end up crippled after subjecting a wound to that kind of neglect. It's the same with a broken marriage. Although repairing the damage is painful, with proper treatment the recovery and healing process can begin. Likewise, we will develop a treatment plan to repair your marriage." Dr. Brightman paused to sip some mineral water. Stephen began wiping his brow and twisting his fingers together in distress.

"I—um—I don't know about all of this," he stammered. "I'm just so torn. It seems like such a hard hill to climb. I really don't know if I'm up to it. I feel so drained, I don't even know if I have the energy."

"It sounds like a lot, doesn't it?" the doctor observed. "When you are both experiencing so many painful emotions, it's hard to know what to do. That tells me it would be best for us to start with individual sessions before we attempt couples' counseling. Each of you is going to need some personal attention, and this will help me see where we need to go. Why don't you look at your schedules and let me know when you're available?"

"Do you have time available for this Thursday around ten?" Stephen asked, looking at the calendar on his phone.

"Sure. I'll set that up." Dr. Brightman booked the appointment.

"Well, that's the very least you can do, Stephen," Sharon snarled, glaring at his phone. "You need to figure this out ASAP, because I am certainly not going to wait around indefinitely for you to decide whether you still want this marriage! I'd like to come in on Wednesday afternoon, Dr. Brightman."

"I have a two o'clock available. Will that work?"

"I'll be here," Sharon replied.

"You're both correct that you need to make an important decision. It's life-altering, and you don't want to make a mistake. Five people's futures are involved here; not just yours, but your boys', as well. I think you're both still in shock, and as you said, it all seems so surreal. The individual sessions will help you recognize whether you want to go forward."

"Well, we need to do something, one way or the other." Sharon tossed her phone into her bag, zipped it closed with an air of finality, and stomped out of the office.

Removing the Mask

Stephen tentatively opened the door to the counselor's office. He braced himself for his private session. Dr. Brightman shifted a vase of peacock feathers to one side of her ornately carved desk, as she welcomed him. "I'm so glad you chose to be here today, Stephen. We really need this opportunity to talk. Please understand that this is all completely confidential and will not be discussed with anyone without your permission. I want to hear your story and where you are at this moment. Please be as honest and open as possible about what you're thinking and how you feel."

For the first time, Stephen actually seemed eager to talk. He leaned forward in his seat, "Do you want me to start with the story of how Holly and I became involved?" Dr. Brightman nodded her assent and Stephen ran a finger under the collar of his golf shirt as if to create a bit more breathing room.

"Holly is a flight attendant who is frequently assigned to my flights. We started getting close about nine months ago. When I first met her, I was attracted to her smile, beautiful blonde hair, and bright blue eyes. On one trip to New York, we were caught in a blizzard, and our plane was grounded for a couple of days. With nothing else to do, the crew had plenty of opportunities to spend time in the bar, talking, drinking, and watching the sports channels. Holly and I enjoyed a lot of the same activities and had many common interests. It was amazing; we seemed so much alike! The more we talked, the more I felt like I'd known her all my life. She was so easy to talk with and was interested in everything I had to say. I hadn't felt that kind of connection with Sharon in a long time. Later that month, the crew had a layover in New Orleans, and we all went out to dinner, then returned to our hotel. Holly and I decided to go into the bar for a few after-dinner drinks. We picked up right where we left off and talked until two a.m., when the bar closed. We decided to continue our discussion upstairs in my room. That was a mistake. Holly's attentions were so flattering! I guess I was kind of blind-sided.

"Things got started right there. We kissed for the first time, and it was hard for me to let her leave. That night as I tried to sleep, all I could think about was how much I wanted to be with her. She later told me that she'd gone to bed that night thinking the same thing. After that, it seemed impossible to contain the attraction that we had for one another, though I'd never intended for things to go that far. I'd always thought I was strong enough never to get caught up in this kind of thing. Holly became my best friend and my lover, an irresistible combination. It was really hard to stay apart. I looked for every opportunity to be with her. And even though I ended the sexual part of the affair after Sharon confronted me about it, I still feel a strong emotional and sexual attraction to Holly. I struggle with it every day.

"I feel so alone now. The emotional connection to Holly is the hardest thing for me to let go. We used to talk several times a day, and I looked forward to that. I miss all of it. So, I'm terribly torn between my feelings for Holly and my love and responsibility to my family. The guilt is unbearable. I find myself in a 'no-win' situation, because no matter what I choose to do, someone I love is going to be hurt. I often think about how miserable Holly felt when I told her I was ending our relationship. She was inconsolable—unable to believe that it was over. In her mind, I was making a heartless choice to walk away from her.

"I can understand Holly's confusion. I'd told her many times how much I wanted to be with her. I've told her since then that having to walk away was one of the hardest things I've ever had to do. Although I've tried to explain what our relationship will do to Sharon and the boys, I doubt if Holly will ever understand the depth of my struggle. She still feels very hurt and contacts me on a regular basis—even though I've asked her not to. She knows better than to text or chat with me by computer of course. But she's become more creative. She says she just can't bear being completely cut off from me. She created a fictitious social-networking identity and asked me to do the same so that we could chat freely online. It's been difficult for me to ignore these invitations, but I have—which only seems to have made things worse. She leaves romantic notes in my inbox at the crew scheduling office where she knows I'll find them.

"I know it's not right, but I read all of her notes and tuck them into my flight manual to reread later. Holly knows exactly what to say to make me feel wanted and desirable. She makes me feel alive again, and I don't know if I want to give that up! It causes me to wonder if my marriage is truly worth saving. I don't want to go back to the way things were." Stephen raised his eyebrows. "That's it in a nutshell. That's where I am. And, it's not a very good place to be."

Dr. Brightman nodded, "You really are conflicted. It's the unfortunate result of being caught in the middle of two strong opposing forces. Your head is telling you to work on your marriage, but your heart is pulling you in an entirely different direction. This is a common dilemma in this kind of situation, and it would be easy to say that your actions caused it, but we can't go back and erase the past."

"I really wish I could just undo everything that's happened."

"And, I wish I had a magic pill for you, but all I can do is tell you what I see happening when someone comes to me about an extramarital relationship. When we factor out the feelings and excitement of the affair, what we see is that it was built on a fantasy. It's easy to enjoy each other with abandon when you don't have the responsibilities of the real world complicating your life. You don't have to worry about obligations like paying bills and taxes, parenting your children, and etcetera. It's like being on a vacation or a holiday. You can forget all about your daily grind for a while and just focus on the pleasure of being together. Also, an affair represents an idealized image of what we hope to find in this new object of our affection. We magnify the good and minimize the bad. We see through rose-colored glasses the manifestation of everything we want in a lover or a mate. Sooner or later, however, the roaches come crawling out of the woodwork, so to speak, exposing hidden flaws.

"Oftentimes, the very things that attract you to a person in the beginning, end up being the things that bother you the most after the mystique evaporates. While you are under the spell of infatuation, you just don't see your lover's faults and problems, nor can you grasp what you might be giving up to follow this fantasy. It's like being in a trance, but the old saying about the grass being greener on the other side of the fence is simply untrue. Once you cross that fence, there are weeds and thorns and bugs and cow pies embedded in that grass that cannot be seen when you're only looking over the fence. You get so narrowly focused on all the pleasant experiences in the isolated world of your affair, that you don't see the obstacles that obscure your view. When you begin to understand this, it helps to break the romantic spell, but of course this doesn't happen overnight. This is because although your perception of the relationship may not be real, your feelings for Holly are very real. I can tell you this only because it's been consistently true over my years of helping people get through things very similar to what you are going through right now."

"Well, that's a slap of reality in the face! It's also hard to believe. It was real to me. I know I didn't imagine it. But the trance, the romantic spell and the isolated world we created together, we experienced all of that. It seemed so right. Holly seemed like everything I'd ever wanted. We had dreams of a life together, but never made any concrete plans as to how it would work."

"I know this is a shock, but sooner or later reality would have come to light on its own," Dr. Brightman confirmed.

Stephen nodded. "Going back to what you mentioned earlier, you're right about my head and heart not being in sync. While I get what you've said, and it makes sense, I still have deep feelings for Holly and I miss her." He smiled, "Are you sure you don't have that magic pill somewhere?"

"Many people ask, and I really wish there were such a medication! I believe you when you say that Holly seemed ideal. Don't you think maybe she represented an escape from your inner struggles and unmet needs? There is the expectation that this new person can fix all that is wrong in your world."

"Yes, and it truly felt like she could," Stephen lamented.

"But you know, each time you reread Holly's notes, you are feeding that fantasy, making it more difficult to let go. If you decide to work on your marriage, you will have to cut off all communication with Holly and destroy the notes and photos you've been keeping. This will be a symbolic act of turning away from Holly; from living in a fantasy world, and turning back toward your marriage, your family, and the reality of life. It will be hard, I know, but you cannot go forward with this emotional triangle intact. You need to choose where to put your time and energy, because it's emotionally draining to hold onto two opposing lifestyles. You need to consider whether it's worth the risk of investing your future in the unknown, or if it's more beneficial to invest yourself in saving your marriage and your family. Only you can make this decision, Stephen. You need to think seriously about what we've discussed today and let me know if you want to continue with our couples' counseling. Do you have any questions before you leave?"

"Right now, I'm flooded with so many thoughts and feelings that I can't even begin to express. What I've heard today has turned me upside down. I have a lot of things to think through that I'd never considered before. I'm overwhelmed. It's exhausting to even think about it."

The counselor nodded. "You're right. I'm not saying it will be easy to work out your marriage problems. But I must caution you that divorce is probably an even bigger mountain to climb. It has its own obstacles to overcome. It will totally and permanently reorganize your and your children's lives, and you'll need to consider that while you're making your choice. You don't want to make a mistake, one way or the other. You want to come out of this having the fewest regrets."

Stephen shook his head vigorously as if to clear his mind. He stood up. "I'm completely blown away by what you've said today. It makes me feel silly and weak that I got caught up in something like this. I'll have to get back with you after I can make some sense out of it."

They exited the office, and the doctor walked out to the reception area with him. "You have a lot on your plate, Stephen. Once you've thought about this, let me know where you want to go from here."

The Other Side of the Story

Sharon gazed out the window. She tried to gather her thoughts. She rummaged through her handbag. She crossed her legs and bounced her foot, as her anger climbed until it flushed her face. She snatched her ever-present water bottle, took a swig, and stowed it back in her purse. About that time, Dr. Brightman entered the reception area and ushered her into the office.

"I'm just so glad to be here!" Sharon began. "You know, I don't think I could have stood this much longer. I'm ready to explode. I can't eat, and I can't sleep. I can't make it through the day without breaking down in tears. Then I get so angry I want to call Holly and tell her off! There's nothing like the feeling of being replaced by a two-bit bimbo to boost a woman's ego," Sharon spouted sarcastically.

"Well, Sharon, I'm glad you're here today too. As you know, I saw Stephen last week. And it's clear that you need a chance to tell your side of the story."

"I feel like such a victim, and I hate this feeling! I've always felt that I was a 'take charge' person, and I don't back down from a challenge. I've practically raised our boys by myself, because Stephen is gone, flying a lot. After the boys started school, I began pursuing my passion for decorating. At first, I helped my friends out and then I began to see the opportunity to start my own interior design business. Stephen was very encouraging. He knew I was getting restless. I like being busy, and I'd found a great outlet for channeling my creative side. I really thought he would be proud of me and respect all that I've accomplished. Instead, he's about to dump me for—of all things—the stereotypical blonde bimbo!" she gushed.

"It's all backward, isn't it?"

"If that's who he really desires, why should I want to chase after him? It makes me wonder if we should even try to work this out. I'm not sure I even want him anymore, Dr. Brightman," Sharon said stiffly. "As a matter of fact, we had a big fight last night, and I asked him to leave. This marriage has obviously become such a farce that it seems like a mockery to live together at this point."

"Sometimes a temporary separation is helpful, Sharon. If there's a lot of anger and hostility, a 'time-out' allows things to settle down a bit and helps everyone get their bearings. If both parties are in counseling with the same counselor and are working toward repairing the damage, I have seen positive results. If they are not in regular counseling together, the outlook is worse since they tend to drift farther apart. For now, though, it seems like you need this time away from each other."

"I don't think I'll trust him ever again. I would always be wondering what he's doing behind my back. How do you build a marriage on that kind of distrust?"

"I know right now it seems impossible, Sharon, but believe me, these things can be worked out—with guidance and support—if you're both committed."

"Well, I know that Stephen still has a lot of feelings for Holly, and I simply can't tolerate having him in the house right now. He needs to stay away until he can figure things out. He tells me he's broken everything off with her, but I know he's depressed about it. You know, I still just don't get it: If he was so unhappy with me, why didn't he talk to me about it instead of sneaking around, playing all those games? Maybe then we could have gotten some help and prevented all this.

"Looking back, his attitude changed decidedly months ago. He became short with me, and nothing I did could please him. He grew cold and distant and our sex life was practically non-existent. I thought he was just under a lot of stress, and I knew that there had been changes at work after his airline merged with another carrier. He used this as an excuse for his cold behavior and irritability, so I tried to cut him some slack. It infuriates me to realize that I believed him, and all the time he was lying to me and sleeping with her!" Sharon's voice trailed off sadly.

"It's a terrible place to be and a hard thing to believe, isn't it? You're probably still in shock about what's happened."

"The strange thing is that I keep asking myself what I did wrong. I replay my faults over and over in my mind, thinking that if I hadn't done this, or if only I had done that, none of this would have happened. I tell myself that I should have known something was wrong, and I question why I let things get this far. Maybe if I had done things differently, we wouldn't be in this mess. I have always been confident about my appearance, and I have a lot of pride in my accomplishments. But I guess none of that mattered to Stephen. He's risked throwing away our marriage and family; and for what? It's just insane."

"Sharon, you're trying to make sense out of what seems like nonsense, but you can't blame yourself for what's happened. Whether or not there was something wrong in your marriage, Stephen made a choice to do what he did. He could have made other choices, if he were that unhappy. Do you understand that?"

"Kind of. I guess I can relate this to how I run my design business. If I have a customer who is unhappy with something, I feel I have a responsibility to work it out with them. I guess that's why I feel responsible for Stephen's dissatisfaction. I feel like I failed, too."

"But, let's be fair here. It's hard to fix something you don't know is broken. What you're engaging in is hindsight. And hindsight is 20/20. Looking back, it's easy to tell yourself what you could have done, but you didn't even know what was really going on. There's no way you can blame yourself. You have to stop that, or you'll find yourself in a deep depression ," Dr. Brightman warned.

"I guess I'm still trying to figure out what happened and why it happened," Sharon admitted. "If there were just some reason I could point to, maybe it would at least explain things. I'm so confused; I don't know what to think. I'm all over the place and still not even sure I want to work this out."

"Why don't you take some time to decide? You can get back to me later."

"I also have no idea where Stephen is on all this either, you know," Sharon replied as she picked up her purse and bid the counselor farewell.

Waking from the Trance

On Monday of the following week, Dr. Brightman received a call from Stephen asking to come in for another individual session, so she set it up for that same afternoon. When he arrived, he went right into what was on his mind.

"Doc, I really needed to get back here. I've spent a lot of sleepless nights since we talked. I toss and turn because I'm so torn about my feelings. I guess you know Sharon threw me out of the house. I'm staying at the extended-stay hotel near our home. I'm really angry about that. Every feeling I have is multiplied in that close space. All these 'if only' thoughts keep whirling around in my head. I keep thinking, 'If only I hadn't done this, I wouldn't be in this shape.' On one hand, I know I need to work on my marriage and do the responsible thing, but, on the other, I still have feelings for Holly. I wonder if I'll ever have another peaceful night's sleep."

"I know you're in turmoil," Dr. Brightman empathized. "Unfortunately, it's going to take some time before you feel better. However, time is on your side, Stephen, if we keep working on this." "It's rough, but it's given me time to think about what you said. I read over Holly's notes one more time; but this time, I read them without wearing my rose-colored glasses, and I did see them a little differently. They said everything I wanted to hear. But this time I tried to separate myself from this so-called fantasy, and they read more like excerpts from a romance novel. It's true: Holly and I never lived in the real world, but it was a wonderful world while it lasted. It allowed me to forget some of the stress I was experiencing, and to enjoy the kind of excitement I no longer felt with my wife. You know, Dr. Brightman, sometimes you just need an escape from reality. But that realization made me wonder if Holly and I would ever have survived the harsh light of everyday life. It became absolutely clear to me that whether Sharon and I fix our marriage, I've got to salvage some kind of relationship for my sons' sake. All I know right now is that I don't want to lose my boys. And that's when I knew I had to burn Holly's notes and delete all of her photos. I needed to follow your recommendation. It was my way of saying goodbye to what I had with Holly. I must admit, I shed more than a few tears as I was doing it—not from the smoke in my eyes, either. I hope this decision will be a turning point for me. I believe that I've got to put my energy and effort into trying to reconcile with Sharon. I know I have to give my marriage another chance."

"And I know how hard that decision was for you, Stephen. Remember, I'm here to help and support you. In your case, I think it's better to try to save your marriage, even if you fail, rather than never try at all."

"Well, that's why I'm here," Stephen replied, his eyes filling with tears.

"It's difficult when your head and heart are in two different places. In time, your heart should catch up with your head. By that, I mean that your thinking brain is still ahead of your emotional brain. You know what you need to do, but your feelings aren't there yet. It will take time for your emotions to catch up, and you'll probably have a few more restless nights. Just try to keep your focus on the decision you've made, and let's take some steps that support it. Let's operate on the premise that as you redirect your focus and act accordingly, your emotional brain will catch up. For a while that might mean that you make a logical decision to work on your marriage, yet still have conflicting emotions."

"It's hard to admit, but I feel a lot of shame. Sharon really didn't deserve any of this. I should have told her I was unhappy with our relationship, but I told myself that everyone gets in a rut after several years of marriage. It seems like we just stagnated." Tears spilled down his face, and he wiped them away quickly in disgust. "I just hope that she can find it in her heart to truly forgive me and that I can finally let go of my feelings for Holly."

"Well, I applaud you for making this decision. I think you and Sharon both deserve an opportunity to work this out. I think it will help if both of you start coming in for joint counseling as soon as possible. Why don't the two of you talk about it and let me know if you would like to make another appointment."

"Sure. I can't stay on this roller coaster much longer. Once we've talked about it and have an agreement, I'll give you a call. It should be in the next couple of days," Stephen added as he rose to leave.

After he'd gone, Dr. Brightman gave a sigh of relief and whispered an earnest prayer for the Sloan couple.

Scraping the Rust Off of Trust

Everything about Sharon's body language underlined her anger with Stephen when they entered the waiting room for their couple session. She walked at a staccato pace, plopped onto the far end of the couch, and began picking at the piped trim on its armrest. When Stephen joined her, she gave him a dirty look, sighed heavily, moved across the room, and continued throwing daggers at him with her eyes. Dr. Brightman read the obvious tension in the room as she greeted them and ushered them into her office.

"Good to see you, Sharon, Stephen. I've had a chance to meet with each of you separately. Now, have you had a chance to talk things over?"

"Well, we did talk, and we want to give our marriage a chance to work. So, we have made that commitment to each other. We'll have to see if these counseling sessions work," Stephen offered stoically.

"I agree. We need to discover whether we can make our marriage work," Sharon began. "Of course, up until recently, I thought it was working just fine, but obviously Stephen didn't think so. And he never bothered to tell me that he was so unhappy until it was too late!"

"Sharon, I wasn't all that unhappy. I just thought that what we were going through was normal after many years of marriage. We were each so busy with our separate lives, it seems like we just slowly drifted apart. I think we both felt unimportant and unappreciated. I know I was resentful, and you probably were too."

"Great—that's really nice," Sharon wisecracked. "You never mentioned any of this to me. If you had just done that much, it would have given us a chance to discuss how we felt, and we might have had a chance to work through it. But no matter how you look at it, nothing excuses what you did. You deliberately followed the path that led to your affair, knowing full well that it was wrong!"

Drift and Re-Bonding

Dr. Brightman rose and approached the whiteboard on the wall, picking up a marker. "Wow, I hear a lot of hurt here, from both of you. But I'm glad you've decided to see what we can do to rebuild your relationship, and I will give you the steps and structure you need." She drew two circles parallel to one another, with a space between them. In the space, she wrote the word "VOID." She drew two arrows on the outside edges of each circle, indicating that the circles were moving away from one another, and then drew an additional circle around each circle.

"What I want to explain to you is that, in part, the affair resulted from the fact that the two of you had already drifted apart. The danger of 'the drift,' as I call it, is subtle and sneaky. You lose your bond and sense of connection. Drift occurs when other priorities take the place of your relationship with each other, and neither spouse gets important needs met.

"Sometimes you don't realize you have lost touch. You feel lonely and empty and may not understand why. We can see how this happened in your situation. It wasn't deliberate, but progressively you lost touch with each other and created separate lives.

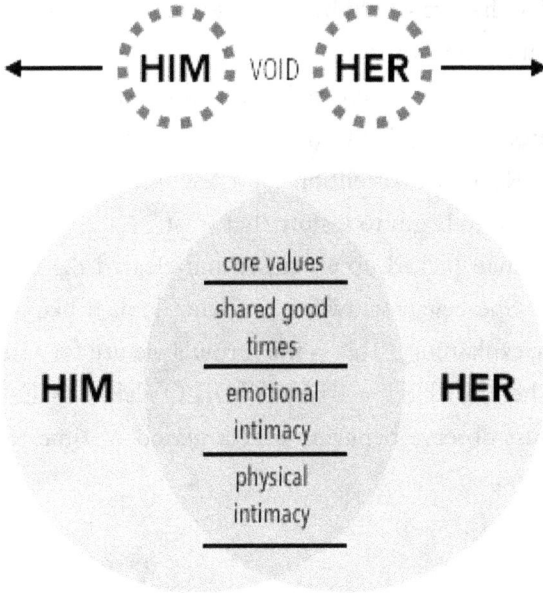

"Your flight schedule, Stephen, Sharon's career, the demands of a busy life, the boys' activities and needs… can you see how this pulled you apart and created a void? It left no quality time for each other. Nature hates a void, and people do, too. So, they attempt to find something or someone to fill that void. Bear in mind, the sense of separation and alienation is a hallmark of 'the drift,' but not an excuse to have an affair. It does make you more vulnerable and is a warning sign for couples to address their frustrations and get help, rather than face the consequences of leaving their longings unaddressed. This is typical of many of the couples I deal with. Do you see what I mean? Does that make sense?"

"That's exactly what happened to us," Stephen and Sharon said in unison.

"Yes. Well, drift is such a subtle process that, as I said, most people never even notice it's what's happening to them. I mentioned when you came in today that we would be taking some important initial steps in restoring that connection.

"First, a major issue to resolve is trust. Your trust has been seriously broken, Sharon, and I'd like to take some time to discuss how to begin to restore it. Really pay attention for a few minutes, while I help you understand how to begin to restore that trust."

Dr. Brightman picked up an eraser and cleared the board for new information. She began scrawling out what looked like a mathematical formula, explaining, "This is the formula we use for assessing trust. As you see here, TRUST = BEHAVIOR OVER TIME. This means that you must observe behavior over a period of time to determine trustworthiness.

Behavior Patterns

"Observing behavior patterns over time is the most reliable way to determine the level of trust. Below, I'm listing the three patterns you should observe…

1) Reciprocity

2) Congruence

3) Boundaries

"Now, let's take a look at the first criteria for trustworthiness.

"Number one: Reciprocity means that there must be an equal commitment and investment from both parties. If one party is putting more effort and energy into the relationship than the other, we say that it is not reciprocal. It's unbalanced. Does that make sense? There has to be a balance."

"So, if Stephen's dragging his feet and not putting forth the necessary effort, this means that he's not fully committed?" Sharon jibed.

"Yeah, and that goes for you, too, Sharon," Stephen snapped.

"That's exactly what this means. Both of you have to do your share of the work that's required here. It's called teamwork. That's why I asked both of you if you have made a decision. If so, you both will need to follow through with it. You will have to demonstrate that you're on the same track—no dragging of feet here!"

Stephen and Sharon nodded in agreement.

"Number two: Congruence means that your words and actions consistently match. If you say you're going to do something, but fail to follow through, you're being incongruent and trust suffers as a result. We know we can't trust people who say things they don't mean. It's evidenced when their actions don't match their words. Would you continue to trust a person like that?"

"Of course not," Sharon replied. "And that's exactly why I don't trust Stephen anymore. He's lied to me again and again."

"Stephen, do you see how important it is that you consistently follow through with what you tell Sharon you will do?"

Stephen stared at the wall, as if trying to distract himself from the doctor's question.

"If there is some definite reason why you cannot follow through on what you've told her, you must let her know ASAP."

"What do you mean?"

"Well, for example, if you say you'll be home at a certain time, and you see that you can't make it, you need to tell her the reason you'll be late. Or, if you say you're going somewhere and your plans change, you need to tell her where you'll be instead."

"Got it," Stephen acknowledged.

"Number three: Boundaries mark a limit. When you set boundaries with a person, and those boundaries are respected, it gives a message that this one is trustworthy and dependable. When our boundaries are violated, we don't feel respected, and therefore we distrust. Boundaries are limits we set to let people know what is unacceptable or intolerable. We need to identify our limits and take responsibility for communicating them to the other person. In your case, we're talking about observing boundaries for several months.

"Trust is such a difficult problem to resolve therapeutically because once it's broken, it takes time to reestablish. There must be a consistent pattern of reciprocity and congruence, along with respect of personal boundaries, if trust is going to be restored. We observe these three criteria over time to determine trustworthiness. Now that I've spelled it out for you, do either of you have any questions?"

"So, if I ask Stephen not to do something, and he continues to do it, he isn't respecting my boundaries, and I can't trust him, right?" asked Sharon. "And what about Stephen's boundaries with Holly? It sounds like we need to discuss those boundaries too."

"Absolutely. That's our next step. You know, Stephen, you will have to maintain strict boundaries with Holly. That means no personal contact whatsoever. Any personal contact will be contradictory to what we're trying to accomplish. Can you make a commitment to do that?" Dr. Brightman queried.

"Yes, I know that, and I am following through on it."

"Sharon, tell Stephen what other boundaries you need in order to feel secure."

"I'd like you to ask crew scheduling to ensure that Holly is not assigned to your flights from now on. I need to know your specific flight schedules and turn-around times. It's those turn-around times that I have the most concern with. If you have to spend the night on a layover, I'd like to FaceTime with you. Don't just text or email me," Sharon insisted with tears in her eyes. "These are the times that will really be hard for me."

Stephen agreed. "I'll make that request and see if it can be arranged. As far as your request for FaceTime during layovers, that's reasonable, and I'll respect that."

"Well, let me know as soon as you find out. I don't want Holly on any of your flights ever again! Also, I need to know your plan for when you land here. You used to stay out for hours, even after I knew your flight had landed. You even turned your phone off to avoid my calls! I want you to come straight home. I need you to agree to those boundaries. Why should I have to worry?"

"You shouldn't have to," Stephen sighed.

"Thank you for your cooperation with this, Stephen," Dr. Brightman interjected. "In future sessions, you can let me know how these three measures of trust are lining up. Here are some handouts with information about the three levels of behavior that lead to trust. You can take these home to study and clarify what we just discussed."

"Speaking of cooperation, I would like to request changing a boundary," Stephen asserted. "I would like to come back home. I feel that since we have made a decision to work on our marriage, I should be home with my family."

"Fair enough," Dr. Brightman interjected. 'But, what do you think about this Sharon?"

"I agree. He should be home if we commit to working together in therapy."

"Is it a done deal then?" Stephen asked.

"It's OK with me, as long as we're moving forward," Sharon replied.

"I think this is a step in the right direction," Dr. Brightman confirmed. "I have one more important thing to discuss with you today. I call it 'shared good times.' A primary step in reconnecting will be enjoying shared good times, but let me define what that means. Stephen, I want you to suggest a time for you and Sharon to be alone to enjoy each other—to just have fun together and relax. There can be no negative, critical, judgmental conversation or attitudes. You'll want to stay away from discussing your problems. We'll do that here in our sessions. Discussing your problems will destroy a shared good time, turning it into a bad time.

"This is based on the 'pleasure principle,' which means that we want to repeat pleasant experiences and avoid unpleasant ones," the counselor explained. "Do you both see why you can't turn this into a negative or unpleasant experience? You must declare this event as a shared good time, so that you have defined it and placed a boundary around it. A time to talk about good times and memories you've had together. A time you can share your dreams and fun things you'd like to do, like travel, go to a concert, or anything else either of you would enjoy.

"Laughter and humor go a long way toward enhancing the fun. Even grown-ups need to take time to laugh and play! If anything turns unpleasant or negative, call a timeout, and redirect your attention. The more good times you have together, the more it reinforces the positive qualities of your relationship. Think about the people you spend time with. Do you enjoy being around a grouch or constant complainer? I don't," Dr. Brightman asserted. "I'm also going to give you a handout of suggestions for shared good times.

"This was an extended session today. I wanted to set up the initial steps to begin this process. I know it's been a lot, but review and talk about the handouts, and we will follow up in the next session," Dr. Brightman instructed as she walked them out of her office.

Clearing the Air and the Mind

"Hi, come on in! How's it been this week?" Dr. Brightman asked, offering smiles, comfy seating, and water bottles. The couple took a moment to settle in, and then Stephen stepped up to the plate.

"It's been so much better this week being back at home—a tremendous relief."

"It's a little uncomfortable for me, but I agree that it's a start." Sharon added.

"I made reservations at Sharon's favorite restaurant Saturday night once I made sure the boys were occupied. It's a quiet, romantic place, and we went there for dinner."

"Did you actually enjoy being together?"

"I know I did," Stephen responded, his blue eyes beginning to twinkle. "Sharon looked beautiful, and I was really attracted to her. She seemed to be in a better place than I'd seen her in for quite a while. It felt great to see that in her. The food and service were excellent too, but the main thing was that I felt happy just being with her." "What about you, Sharon?" the doctor asked.

"It was a nice surprise for me to see that we could actually sit down and enjoy being together. It's like I just put my hurt away in the back of my mind for a while and relaxed. I didn't have to think about it for a few hours. I know this doesn't solve our problems, but it was nice to have a brief respite from our struggle. We did what you said, and it was really pleasant to remember some wonderful memories we have with each another," Sharon said with a slow smile creeping over her face.

"It sounds like the two of you actually enjoyed following these directions, and I applaud you for that! Are you ready to take a look at how you're doing with rebuilding trust?"

"We went through the handouts you gave us on trust, and it all makes sense, even though I know it's going to take some time and focus. I just hope I can measure up," Stephen added.

"I'm glad we have the handouts," Sharon agreed. "It's nice to have some reminders, because it's hard to stay focused when all trust has been broken."

"Yeah, I can tell that it's going to take a heck of a lot of effort to restore your trust in me. You said you'd never trust me again, and that really hurt."

"Oh, boohoo! I'm so sorry that hurt you. That must have been very difficult," Sharon rolled her eyes.

"Restoring trust is difficult, no matter where you stand," Dr. Brightman interjected. "So, let's review our formula for trust. Remember, we said that it's a function of observing behavior over time. What have you observed about reciprocity in your relationship? Are you putting forth a mutual effort into working this out?"

"Well, it looks like it at this point, but I'm constantly on guard with him," Sharon replied. "I'm still afraid he'll bail and run back to Holly."

"Well, I wouldn't be here working on this if that's what I planned to do. That should demonstrate some commitment on my part, don't you think?" Stephen retorted.

"What about congruence?" Dr. Brightman asked. "Remember, congruence is when your words and actions match. How do you two feel about that?"

"Well, Stephen says he loves me and finds me sexy and attractive. But I'm sure he must have said the very same things to Holly, so I don't know where that leaves us. I do notice now that he is more physically affectionate with me. He gives me hugs, and instead of sitting across the room, he sits with me on the couch now."

"Well, Sharon, you've really surprised me! Stephen replied. "I can't wait to be near you. You've been initiating intimacy more than I ever remember, and I love that you're wearing the sexy lingerie that I bought you years ago. They'd never come out of the drawer before now!"

"I've been trying to entice you, so you won't be so inclined to look back," Sharon lifted an eyebrow.

"Whatever your motivation, keep it up!" Stephen laughed appreciatively.

"It's not funny!" Sharon snapped, "I really shouldn't have to try to win you back."

"That's true, Sharon," Dr. Brightman reassured her. "You'll have to decide in your heart how much affection you want to give as you and Stephen work through these early stages. You will have to determine how much closeness or distance you prefer, and you'll both have to respect that.

"Let's move on to your boundaries. How's that working for you? Sharon expressed an emphatic demand that you cut off all communications—in person and electronically—with Holly. She also made some requests about communicating your whereabouts and handling your flight assignments."

"I know cutting off all connection with Holly is non-negotiable, and I'm committed to that. I also believe I'm respecting your boundaries about my schedule and my daily activities. Is that right, Sharon?"

"Yeah. So far, you're doing okay at keeping me up to speed. But what about requesting Holly is taken off your crew scheduling?"

"I've looked into it, but I learned that I can't really dictate to crew scheduling who is assigned to my routes. I'm going out of my way to avoid flying with her though. I really don't want to see her anyway. It would just be too awkward."

"Yeah. After you've dirtied all the water in the pool, it wouldn't be pleasant to go back and swim in it, would it, Stephen?" Sharon sniped.

Dr. Brightman spoke up, "I know you're angry, Sharon. So we've got to work through that. It will involve several steps. But first, I want you to learn some important communication skills. Good communication is the beginning to any healing process.

"Couples talk in codes. The message gets confused: You say one thing, but the other hears something else. Then you make assumptions about the meaning. You suppose you know the other's motives and intentions and fill in the lack of understanding with your own perceptions.

This is like mind reading, and it's impossible. It creates defensiveness and blame, which sidetracks from the real issue. Hasn't that happened to you?"

Sharon and Stephen both nodded.

"Don't assume you know anyone's motives or intention. Ask a question such as: 'Are you doing that because...?' When you turn an assumption into a question, it doesn't feel so intrusive to the other person. Can you see that by asking a question, it changes the message?"

"Sharon does that all the time. She assumes she knows what's in my head, what I'm thinking and feeling," exclaimed Stephen. "She doesn't bother to ask."

"Yes, it's so easy to misunderstand each other. Multiple research studies have indicated that about 93% of the message we get when someone is speaking doesn't even come from words. That means only about 7% of what we hear actually comes from the words. It's easy for a person to say one thing and for the other person to hear something else. So, the conversation gets off-track right from the beginning. Now listen to this: 55% of the message comes from non-verbal cues, such as eye contact, facial expression, proximity, body posture, and hand and arm movements. Isn't that amazing? These visual cues are more powerful than words. You can see why we miss so many cues when we're talking on the phone or texting. And here's another one: 38% of the message comes from tone of voice, and volume or rapidity of speech. An angry or sarcastic tone, a loud voice, or rapid-fire questioning communicates emphatic messages that overrule words.

After writing this on the marker board, Dr. Brightman gave them a handout.

"What you're saying is that sometimes the words aren't even that important. We have misunderstandings because we read cues more than the words," Sharon observed. "I think that happens a lot!"

"So, you can say nice things while giving someone a grimacing look?" asked Stephen, giving Sharon a sidelong glance.

"Yeah. You do that all the time!"

"Right, and I guess you don't? I see the withering looks you give me when you say you're okay, and you really aren't," Stephen accused.

Dr. Brightman took control again, "This is a major reason a discussion might never get off the ground. It descends into negative feedback loops which escalate emotions. When your emotions start to overwhelm you, take a **timeout** as when you are really angry. It can be anywhere from twenty minutes to twenty-four hours. Then open the discussion again. Anything longer than twenty-four hours is considered 'stonewalling.' Take a walk, go listen to some music, putter in the garden. Do whatever calms you down because escalating emotions causes your heart rate to increase, and research says that when your heart rate reaches one hundred beats or more per minute, you can't communicate in a logical, rational manner. Emotions take over and hijack the discussion. A timeout gives you a chance to cool off and sort things out."

"That might be easier said than done. Sharon, when you get upset you follow me around fuming and fussing, demanding answers from me," Stephen complained agitatedly. "Then I get frustrated and start yelling back, and things just escalate from there!"

"That's exactly what I'm talking about here, Stephen. You get caught up in a negative feedback loop, these deeply rutted paths of negative communication, which keep you in a cycle of escalating tension and strife. Without a timeout, you escalate and get easily overwhelmed emotionally."

"I just hate it when you shut me down," Sharon exclaimed. "I have all these pent-up feelings, and you just don't want to hear about them!" Sharon exclaimed.

"But can you see, Sharon, that this approach gets you nowhere?" Dr. Brightman offered. "Of course, you should be able to talk and express your feelings. I will soon give you a tool for doing just that. However, you don't have the tools right now, so I would like for you both, for the time being, to declare a DMZ—demilitarized zone—in your discussions about the affair. You will continue to become trapped in these toxic emotional loops until you learn some more basic communication tools.

"I will introduce them next week. So, don't worry, you'll have plenty of opportunities to express your feelings," the doctor promised. "One final tip I want to give you about improving communication is the use of a **reflection**. This involves making sure you really hear each other correctly. For example, when Sharon speaks, and there is some misunderstanding, then Stephen should reflect back what he heard by saying, 'What I heard you say was _____.' If Sharon says, 'That's right,' then you've heard what she intended. But if she says 'No, you don't get it,' she needs to repeat what she said. Stephen, you then repeat it back to her, to show her you got her meaning. Or if you say something, and you feel misunderstood, ask Sharon, 'What did you hear?' That will get you on the same page."

"That sounds kind of silly," Stephen said sheepishly. "That would make me sound like I'm kind of stupid or something."

"Well, once again, it's all in your tone of voice and non-verbal cues. Both of you will have to realize that by your tone and expressions, you're sending a message. That's why it's important to know when to use **inflections**. This one skill can quickly steer the course of the conversation in a positive direction. This is plenty for today. Consult your handouts; they will help. Continue with your shared good times. Sharon, it's your turn to plan the next one. Watch your trust levels, and I'll ask you for a report. Watch out for negative feedback loops, and take a timeout when there is too much tension. I'll show you how to process escalating tension in our next session; otherwise it can resurface as ammunition in future arguments. Plan on spending some extra time with me next week, because I have a lot of information, and I don't want to give it to you piece-meal. Are you okay with that?" "Sure. What have we got to lose?" Stephen shrugged.

"See you next week, same time, same place," Sharon chimed in.

Building Bridges

"Tell me about the shared good time you planned, Sharon."

"Well, Doctor," Sharon began. "I decided to follow through on my idea to bring some humor back into our marriage. So, I took Stephen to an open mic night at the local comedy club. We'd never been before, so we didn't know what to expect. The comedians and locals who took the stage were really funny, and we both laughed so hard, we lost our breath a few times! It's been a long time since either of us found something so hilarious. Especially when we heard that lady trying to describe her husband making pickles..." Sharon covered her face with her hands and started giggling.

"Stop!" Stephen stammered, blushing and snickering. "Dr. Brightman doesn't want to hear about that—I hope."

"Oh, I don't know, I've been known to enjoy the occasional pickle story. But I'm much happier hearing that you're beginning to enjoy one another! Remember, we talked about regaining trust. What have you learned about trustworthiness?"

"Well, those three markers you gave us helped a lot in measuring where we are. But for me, I know it's going to be a long time before I can fully trust Stephen again."

"But I've been respecting the boundaries we set up!" Stephen interjected.

"You do seem to be doing okay at that, as far as I can tell. But I wonder whether you're really committed to our marriage or just going through the motions. You obviously weren't committed before, so how can I believe you now?"

Stephen shrugged. "I'm here for every session, aren't I? And I'm following through. Can't you see that?"

"So, Dr. Brightman, I guess we're making progress, however slowly," Sharon sighed, her voice trailing off.

"This is a good time, then, to talk about what is most important to you," the doctor explained. "I want to talk about something called core values. Core values connect you through the traditions and beliefs you hold most dear. Your common values form a vision for the marriage and life you want to live. Without a common vision, you will be at cross-purposes and will pull further away from each other. We could say you are unequally yoked.

"As you can see now, the distance between the two of you had been growing and dividing you long before Stephen's affair. The two of you had been drifting apart. We need to draw you back toward your shared vision that lines up with your marriage and family values.

"Right now, I'd like for each of you to tell me two things: First, tell me one of your most cherished memories as a couple. Then, I want you to tell me about a mutual interest or a value that you have in common. Take a few minutes and jot down your thoughts. It will help you to remember what attracted you to one another in the beginning."

The couple took the notepads that Dr. Brightman handed them and began jotting down some notes. Sharon looked up when she finished, and Dr. Brightman gestured for her to begin. She took a deep breath and cleared her throat.

"We always wanted to start a family. Parenting our children together was a priority for us. We wanted to give them the best life could offer. For me, the greatest day of my life was the day our first son was born. Fortunately, it was a rather easy birth. Stephen was with me the whole time, and I drew on his strength and support. We both cried tears of joy when we saw Trent. When I held him in my arms, I thought I had done the most incredible thing by bringing him into the world."

Dr. Brightman smiled as the two of them savored the memory. "Thanks for sharing that. What about you, Stephen? Can you think of a memory you'd like to add?"

"That was tops for me too—miraculous. One of my favorite memories of us? The first thing that comes to mind is our love of watching our boys compete in sports. I'm so proud of their effort and determination. I want to be the kind of father they know they can count on, one who inspires them to achieve their goals. Lately, I've been so distracted with other things. I realize I need to spend more of my time making memorable moments with Sharon and the boys.

"Thanks for your thoughts, Stephen. It's obvious your family is most important to you. These values define your goals. Your commitment to raising your boys and giving them all the opportunities you can will hold you and Sharon together, as a common bond. You both want the best for your children."

"It's true. We are both devoted to our boys, and we don't want to destroy our family," Emotion shook Sharon's voice. "I know they would be devastated if we divorced."

"They really would be," Stephen agreed.

"Now, are you ready for the next step in rebuilding your marriage? If you are, then it's time we looked into the process of healing the emotional pain caused by the affair," Dr. Brightman explained, broaching the sensitive subject. "No one wants to see or hear how we've hurt others, but the way out of this pain is to be able to work through it together.

"While most people are, of course, challenged by facing intense emotions, you should know that men, in particular, often have difficulty dealing with any hurt, anger, and suffering they have caused and don't want to be reminded of it. Many men opt to retreat by avoidance or become hostile and defensive. The men I've worked with often say they would do anything to fix this, but they don't know how, so they just either get angry when an unpleasant subject is brought up or they run away ."

Dr. Brightman paused for Stephen's response and was surprised when Sharon spoke up instead.

"I don't want to rehash everything that's happened. I'm afraid I'll just get upset all over again and lose whatever progress I've made so far."

"You think you're dreading it? I'm certainly not looking forward to digging into all of this either!" Stephen exclaimed. "I've said I'm sorry a dozen times. Can't we just move on from here?"

"Let me assure you both, this isn't about rehashing. "This process is designed to help you resolve your feelings, not make them worse. We can't simply ignore the fact that this has been a traumatic time in your life. It has had a catastrophic effect on your marriage that cannot be denied. You can't sweep it under the rug. It will just come back to haunt you. Remember the analogy I shared about the broken leg?

"Try to relax and let me explain how this works. This is what the process will look like." Then she sketched a diagram on the whiteboard.

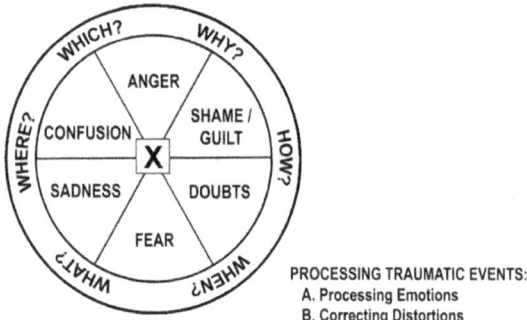

PROCESSING TRAUMATIC EVENTS:
A. Processing Emotions
B. Correcting Distortions

"This diagram is a representation of the pain and emotional stress this affair has caused. We can call this a traumatic event in your life. We define trauma as '**an emotional shock that has a lasting psychological effect.**' When an event causes an emotional shock, it requires specific measures to reduce or eliminate any damaging psychological effects. As you can see from our diagram, there is a lot of anger, sadness, fear, confusion, guilt and shame. This creates internal turmoil, and can eventually make things even worse. The strong temptation is to just avoid dealing with it altogether, but unresolved anger can lead to resentment, bitterness, and even attacks of rage. Prolonged sadness can lead to depression, while unchecked fear can lead to anxiety and panic attacks. Holding onto guilt and shame can cause self-condemnation, regret, and remorse. Do you see what I mean? These exhausting emotions can use up to 85% of your mental energy."

"Since the affair, it seems that all I can think about is what's happened," Sharon confessed. "It occupies my thoughts constantly; again and again my mind wanders into the worst possible scenarios. I can't seem to concentrate on what I'm doing during the day. I get so angry at Stephen just thinking about all of this, I want to scream and yell at the slightest provocation! At other times, I can't seem to stop crying. Then I get scared because my life has been turned upside down, and I can't see where it's going from here." Sharon sobbed, reaching for the tissues. "It all just keeps flooding through my mind. I thought I was doing better, but obviously I'm not."

"You're describing the impact of a traumatic experience, Sharon," Dr. Brightman explained. "Try to think for a moment how the events of 9/11 and their aftermath impacted everyone. That was trauma; all the anger, confusion, grief, fear, and even guilt Americans felt when that happened. You can see in this diagram how the human brain cycles through painful emotions again and again as it struggles to put a traumatic event into some kind of perspective. After 9/11, we tried to make sense of this national catastrophe with whatever information we could gather. And every time the media flashed the images of those crashing towers, the painful feelings came rushing back. That is a tragic example of how a traumatic event can be triggered by a word or image. That's the kind of damage trauma does to our minds. It drastically changes our thoughts and intensifies our feelings," Dr. Brightman explained.

Sharon nodded. "I can relate to that. For me, the trigger is seeing things in a romantic movie or TV show. I can't watch one anymore without thinking 'that's exactly where Stephen and Holly were just a few weeks ago.' I don't know if I'll ever be able to relax and enjoy a movie again. I get a knot in my stomach every time I see one of those images. Even certain songs bring up strong feelings."

"Those triggers are exactly what we've been talking about. They can be very intrusive; it's like they just force themselves into your mind."

"Exactly," Sharon responded.

"Well, romantic movies aren't my favorite pastime right now, either, for what it's worth," Stephen interjected, rubbing at the scruff of his chin.

"I know it seems hard to believe right now, but this pain will loosen its grip if you two are able to talk about the impact and are able to listen compassionately and empathetically to each other. For now, you can both relax."

How the Brain Works

Dr. Brightman had a calming smile. "I'm going to use a specifically designed structure for this recovery process, so right now, bear with me while I go into teaching mode for a few moments." Both Sharon and Stephen took deep breath and focused their attention on what she had to say.

"Let me give you a very simple overview about how the brain functions. Actually, we have three brains in one—a triune brain—meaning we have three basic functional systems that are a part of the brain. We have the 'sensing brain,' which incorporates sight, sound, smell, touch, and taste. Then we have our so-called '**THINKING** brain' located in the region of our foreheads. Here we see a diagram of the thinking brain, or pre-frontal cortex, and it is primarily responsible for intellectual reasoning and decision-making. Finally, we have our 'EMOTIONAL brain' located in the central area of the brain, where emotions are processed. Of course, there are interconnections throughout all parts of our brains, but for our purposes, we are going to focus on two respective centers.

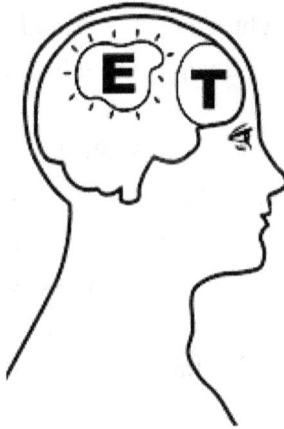

"Remember the impact of emotional trauma drains the brain's energy by about 85%, leaving only 15% of your brain's energy available for other tasks. That is what you were just describing, Sharon, when you were talking about your confusion, emotional exhaustion and inability to focus."

"Ouch, this gives me a headache!" Sharon moaned.

"I'm sure it does, so let's look at why that might be. Your attempt to explain why the affair happened is primarily processed in your thinking brain, while the painful feelings are primarily processed in your emotional brain, sapping your mental energy. Are you understanding, what I'm saying?"

"This is all new information to me, but it makes some sense, I think," Sharon replied.

"I think I get it. The picture you drew on the board really helps me put this into perspective," Stephen added.

"That's what I'm here to do, and I'd like to start with you, Sharon." Sharon nodded and leaned forward attentively. "I'm sure you've tried many times to explain to yourself how and why this happened, right? This is an example of how the thinking brain operates. You want to make sense of why things happen."

"Absolutely. I've thought about it over and over again, wondering how we got here and why." Sharon circled her finger above her head to indicate the confusion.

"And what conclusions have you reached?"

Sharon turned to Stephen, "Well, my first conclusion as to why this happened is that I am obviously not enough for you. I'm not attractive, interesting, or sexy enough. I wonder how I became someone you found so unappealing that you turned to someone else. I think I must have done something to cause all of this. I also wonder why I can't let this go. Surely I should be able to cope better than this and move on with my life. I must be a truly miserable soul to fall into this cycle of self-pity and stay stuck in it."

"You know, Sharon, I hear this kind of thing from a lot of others in your situation," the doctor pointed out. "To move past this, it is very important that we correct any distorted thinking patterns you have. Believe me, you've got plenty of distortions! So, let me address what I've heard you say. You think you must be responsible. That's a distortion. You didn't drive Stephen to do this, and you are in no way responsible for the choice he made. Even if it were true that Stephen felt the way you assume he did, he still had no excuse for stepping over the line, so you can't blame yourself. There were plenty of other options he could have chosen, like talking to you about his frustration or going to counseling. But he chose not to do that. This is about him, not you." "Are you following me?"

"It's certainly a relief to hear that, but it's going to be hard to hold onto that realization the next time I start thinking I'm the one who caused him to meet his needs outside of our marriage," Sharon answered, lowering her eyes.

"It's going to be up to you to correct your thinking whenever you start blaming yourself. You'll have to take charge of that by saying to yourself, 'Sharon, you are not responsible for Stephen's behavior. Sharon, Stephen is responsible for his choices, and you can't control his behavior.' And according to recent research, speaking your own name gives a commanding message to your brain," Dr. Brightman noted as Sharon jotted the suggestions down.

"As far as condemning yourself for being overwhelmed by your emotions and defining it as self-pity, that also is a symptom of distorted thinking. It's normal to be emotionally overwhelmed when devastating events happen, and you've been in crisis mode. That's not the same as feeling sorry for yourself. Anyone would feel crushed by your circumstances. It turns your life upside down. So again, you're going to say to yourself, 'Sharon, you don't have self-pity. Sharon, you are feeling normal emotions, and it is okay to be sad and hurt and angry when someone has deceived and betrayed you,'" Dr. Brightman took a deep breath and sipped from her water bottle, then turned to Stephen.

"How about it? How would you explain your behavior?"

"Well, I think I made the excuse that you were too busy with your own life and interests and didn't appreciate me, Sharon. I felt like I was a low priority, and I didn't like it. So, I justified my relationship with Holly as my right to the companionship and affection I lacked with you. I gave myself permission to indulge my fantasies. I didn't realize it would go this far. It just happened."

"This kind of thing doesn't just happen," Sharon corrected, giving Stephen a withering look. "You can't make the excuse that it wasn't your intent to get that involved. You didn't stop yourself. You gave in to your own selfish desires and indulged your fantasies."

"I guess I have to admit that's what happened. I got caught up in a whirlwind and didn't stop when I knew I should have. I thought I could get away with it, and no one would be hurt. I didn't think about the consequences at the time."

Dr. Brightman agreed. "You're right, Stephen. When you became so absorbed in the emotional euphoria of an affair, the thinking brain wasn't working too well. But you do understand that your behavior was of your own making, not Sharon's, right? Using your anger and resentment toward her as an excuse is unacceptable. You had other options. And you thought no one would be hurt? How's that working out?" Dr. Brightman arched an eyebrow emphatically.

"Don't rub it in, Doctor!" Stephen exclaimed in exasperation. "I know I'll be paying for this for the rest of my life. Sharon still threatens me with divorce. With hindsight, my mistake is obvious, but I didn't see it at the time. I was blind."

"Bingo!" Dr. Brightman exclaimed. "See how important it is that we correct distorted thinking? It's impossible to get past a problem when your thinking is wrong and you're dealing with overwhelming emotions. It drives us down the wrong path, making it difficult to recover."

"Yeah, well, I would define all of this as a mental tsunami that has just about flattened me. It stretched me to my limits," Stephen replied with a heavy sigh.

"That's an excellent description! And speaking of mental tsunamis, you both need a break. I'm sure you'll be relieved to hear that this session is over! But before we leave, I want to mention something we'll be discussing next week. I'll be showing you some more ways to help you work through the emotional pain you're experiencing.

"This session, too, will require a little extra time, as I'll need to teach you how to use the exercise before we try it together. You both went through a lot today, so try to catch your breath, relax, and remember to schedule a shared good time. Good work!" Dr. Brightman exclaimed as they walked out of the office.

Smoke Signals & Mirrors

The next week, Sharon and Stephen entered Dr. Brightman's office, exchanging their customary greetings. They pulled out their cell phones and briefly showed photos of their sons from the previous weekend's soccer games and baseball finals.

"I'm so glad you've been sharing this family time together! Looks like everybody had a good time," the doctor commented.

"Yes, but we're still scheduling our shared good times with each other, as well," Stephen reminded.

"And how are things going with the two of you?" Sharon began, "Well, I'm still angry about being betrayed and lied to. I've been furious with Stephen for making me feel so humiliated and stupid. I conjure up these scenarios of the two of them having wild sex, and I wish I could stop these images from incessantly tormenting me. I have no idea what you're thinking anymore, Stephen. You've been very quiet all week, like you're in your own little world, and I'm the one left trying to deal with all of this on my own. I want to talk, but you're reluctant. And I'm angry about not having any answers. This whole thing is like a nightmare to me, and I can't seem to wake up."

"That's it exactly, Sharon," the counselor responded. "Of course, you would feel that way. I'm sorry you've been put in this position and are having to suffer for it. In this office, it will be safe for you to express all the feelings that are bombarding you."

Dr. Brightman took a breath and turned to Stephen. "How about you, Stephen? What's been going on with you this week?"

He cleared his throat. "Well, this has been a tough week. I've really been dreading this session. Honestly, I'm completely lost. I feel so helpless. I've really just shut down, and don't know what else to do. Sometimes I think we are moving forward, but then I feel we're going backward again."

"We're going to do whatever we can to turn this around," Dr. Brightman emphasized supportively. "I can't stand the way it makes me feel, Sharon!" The words seemed to be bursting out of Stephen. "I've repeatedly told you I'm sorry. Why can't we move on? You make it worse by insisting that I recount all the details of what happened between Holly and me, particularly about the sex. You are absolutely relentless about it! You continually hound me for the details of everything Holly and I did," he blurted out in frustration.

"Oh, boohoo! What do you think I've been through?" Sharon snapped, their magic weekend memories dispelled. "I think I have a right to know exactly what happened. You've got to come clean. What was sex like with Holly? Was sex better with her?"

Stephen shot Dr. Brightman a quizzical look.

"It's typical to want know the intimate details of what happened, but the more details Sharon knows, the more it will load her mind with memories that will haunt her. I'm going to give you an important piece of information, Stephen. Sharon, it's equally important that you hear this, as well. Too many details, particularly sexual scenarios, can prolong your recovery effort. Any intimate details can spontaneously trigger more painful thoughts and feelings. Stephen, Sharon could be having a terrific day, only to have it ruined instantly by seeing or hearing something that reminds her of any details you've revealed to her.

"You should discuss the affair only in the most general terms, with as few details as possible," Dr. Brightman cautioned, looking at each of them in turn.

"What do you mean?" Sharon asked. "He needs to come clean about all of his sordid acts. I have a right to know!"

"And what do you hope to accomplish with this knowledge, Sharon?" Dr. Brightman quizzed.

"Well, at least, it might help me to know why I'm so undesirable to him. Why he found her more exciting than me."

"What do you have to say about that, Stephen?"

"Talking about the specifics just brings up memories I'm trying to forget. I don't need to be dragged back into all that," Stephen stammered pleadingly.

"Both of you have just made my point! The more those intimate details are revealed, the more they will be remembered and relived. They will be harder to leave in the past. Those specifics will be triggers that continue to provoke strong negative emotions."

Sharon didn't seem pleased with that last point. Turning toward Stephen, she noted that he seemed visibly relieved.

Since neither cared to discuss the subject further, they moved the session forward. "This is a good time to introduce how to **process those feelings** you've described. I'll be in my 'teacher' mode again for a few moments, so bear with me. Since our feelings drive our behavior, you can see how neglecting your feelings could set you up for destructive behaviors.

"The **processing skill** allows us to express these feelings without causing **negative feedback loops** of escalating anger and misunderstanding. Please listen carefully to my instructions, because what I'm about to discuss is very counter-intuitive. It's not at all what you're used to doing and will seem unreasonable at first. This is a specific communication skill that engages both the speaker and listener in clearly defined roles. It will seem scripted at first, but you will get used to it."

Dual Brain Processing

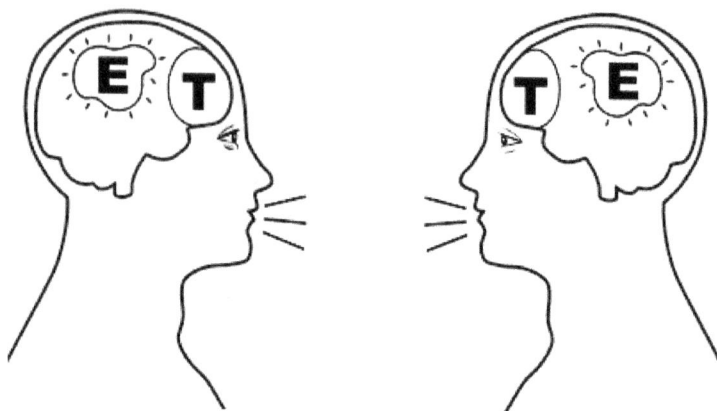

"The concept is simple, but the application is not particularly easy. It focuses on the *impact* of the behavior, rather than the behavior itself. It's too easy to get defensive about our own behavior, make excuses, or say, 'Sorry, I didn't mean to; it wasn't my intent to hurt you.' However, you did what you did, whether you intended to or not, and that had an impact. The challenge will be to stay grounded and focus on listening to the impact of your behavior as expressed by feelings."

"Remember, we used the concept of trauma, to define the turmoil you're going through. I have another visual diagram I'd like to share with you that best illustrates the impact of this trauma and the psychological and emotional damage it does." Dr. Brightman gave the Sloans two handouts detailing the instructions for processing, then she began drawing a diagram of two facial profiles on her whiteboard. Inside the heads, she sketched the shape of a brain, labeling the thinking areas and emotional processing areas.

"When a person is angry, which part of the brain do you suppose is most active?"

"Well, I guess that's when the emotional brain is most active," Sharon stated.

"That's right, and where does that leave the thinking brain?"

"Does that leave the thinking brain compromised, since so much of the mental energy is going to the emotional brain?" Stephen asked.

"Right, again! So, does it make a lot of sense to speak to the thinking brain, when this area is suffering from energy deprivation? Do you think it does any good to make excuses, give explanations or defensive arguments if the person's mind can't process rationally when it's flooded with emotions? You do realize that the more emotionally flooded we become, the less rational we become. Are you following me?"

"You're saying the more emotional we are, the more irrational we become?" Stephen asked.

"Yes. How can a person think clearly when he or she is emotionally flooded? The emotions overwhelm the thinking," Dr. Brightman explained. "We've all said or done something in a fit of anger that we regretted once we calmed down. Our thinking brain was temporarily hijacked by our emotional brain."

"Oh, yes. Been there, done that!" Stephen exclaimed.

Sharon nodded, "I can relate to that too."

"So, let's say you have become very emotional and someone says, 'You need to calm down; it's not that bad. You're making a mountain out of a molehill.'"

"Sounds familiar! You do that to me all the time, Stephen, thinking you can shut me down," Sharon interjected.

"Does that work, when he does that?"

"Absolutely not; it makes me madder than ever!"

"So, he defeated his own purpose, right?"

"Well, what in the world am I supposed to do?" Stephen asked. "She gets so upset, it frustrates me, and I need to do something, but what?"

"You do just the opposite of what you think you should do," the doctor replied. "Instead of telling her to calm down and get over it, you validate the feelings she is expressing."

"Okay. But she's not just expressing her feelings—she's yelling and screaming at me!" Stephen protested.

"Right, but if you follow me, I can help you respond in a manner that will calm her down. This is what I mean about the **processing skill** being counterintuitive. Instead of trying to shut down her feelings, you **validate** them."

"But, that doesn't make sense! Won't that just give her the right to continue yelling and screaming at me?"

"I'll deal with Sharon's yelling and screaming in a just a minute. But follow along with me for now. You stay with the feelings by **validating** her anger: 'I understand that you're angry about that.' Then, **empathize** with her. Put yourself in her shoes for a moment and say how you would feel: 'I'd feel the same way if you did that to me.' Then you need to tell her you're sorry, only after you let her know you understand and can empathize with her."

"Whatever! I've already told her I'm sorry dozens of times, and it doesn't do any good," Stephen muttered.

"Well, let me introduce you to the ReVEAL process for dealing with this kind of conflict. ReVEAL stands for a series of steps you can take that will help you deal with the problem."

Re—Reflect back the feeling

V—Validate the feeling

E—Empathic Response

A—Apologize

L—Lean into the need

"What you did didn't work, Stephen, because you left out the first three steps, and you don't sound sincere, so she doesn't believe you.

"**First,** you didn't REFLECT back to her what you heard her say.

"**Second,** you didn't reassure her that her anger was VALID and understandable.

"**Third**, you didn't EMPATHIZE with her, letting her know you'd feel the same way in similar circumstances.

"So, when you are in a hurry to say you're sorry, it falls flat. She doesn't believe you really care or understand how she feels. What she hears is that you just want her to shut up, forget the whole thing, and move on. Get it?"

"That's right!" Sharon exclaimed. "You say you're sorry, but you don't show any understanding or compassion. I might begin to believe you actually cared, if you responded even close to what Dr. Brightman has described."

Stephen looked dumbfounded. "You mean, that's what I should have been doing all this time?" The counselor nodded. "That's what will help, when she's upset. You need to engage with her like we just discussed. It's in your handout. Process through it with her. Take charge of the situation. But that's not all: **fourth**, APOLOGIZE. And **fifth**, after making a sincere apology, LEAN INTO THE NEED. Ask her, 'Sharon, what do you need from me right now? How can I make things better for you?' Now she is more calm and can tell you what she needs from you. You've engaged her thinking brain."

"Back to you, Sharon. It's now up to you to think about what you need from Stephen at that moment. It needs to be something he can then do for you; give you reassurance, give you a hug, commit to continued counseling, or whatever will make you feel better."

"This is making my head spin. It's so different," Stephen sighed weakly.

"Too bad! I like what I'm hearing!" Sharon jibed.

"Now, wait a minute, Sharon," Dr. Brightman cautioned. "Remember: Turnabout is fair play! You'll need to follow this exercise when Stephen is upset, as well."

"You mean I have to use this same process with him, even though he's the one who caused all of this?" Sharon asked with disgust.

"I'm afraid so. Even though he caused it, he's still getting a backlash of feelings. It's affected both of you, although in different ways."

"Truer words were never spoken," Stephen muttered. "I feel the impact every day!"

"I'm just trying to assimilate all this information. It's so different, it's making my head swim, too," Sharon chimed in.

"And, if it works, I think it will be a miracle!" Stephen added doubtfully.

"Research shows that this processing skill is very effective, when used appropriately. It's a matter of learning a new type of communication. Let's go through it and briefly discuss how we will begin next week's session.

"First, you identify a particular situation you want to process. Sharon, you will begin by describing the emotional impact by labeling your emotions using your Vocabulary List of Feelings (see page 197). Say, 'I felt/feel _____ (use 3 or 4 feeling words) when _____ (the situation that happened).' These statements should be very short and succinct. People mistakenly think that the more they talk, the better they will be understood. The fact is, however, just the opposite is true. People tend to 'trance out' if you give them too much information all at once. The most important part of your job, Sharon, is to make sure that Stephen correctly hears what you're trying to say, by **reflecting** it back to you.

"Sharon, anytime you feel flooded with doubt, confusion, anger, or escalating emotions that will be your signal that you need to process your feelings. You will need to talk about the impact by putting words to feelings. Then Stephen's responsibility is to listen and respond according to the steps I have provided for you (ReVEAL). Sharon will need this more often at first, but she will feel incrementally better each time you walk her through the step, slowly and methodically, reducing her emotional distress. You should be prepared to go through these steps any time she feels emotionally overwhelmed, realizing that this is a route to healing the emotional damage."

Dr. Brightman paused to give them more handouts before she continued, "It's your responsibility, Stephen, to listen to the pain you have caused her, and understand its impact."

"I sure hope I can do this," he groaned .

"I know that was a lot to put on your plate. But as you experiment with this, you will see how well it works."

"Well, I hope this knocks some sense into his head," Sharon commented disgustedly.

"Sounds like you're not too sure about this either. Don't worry, we will practice this in our sessions and I will be coaching you. Continue to build on your shared good times and remind each other of your favorite memories as a couple. Be careful about making assumptions, and ask for clarification if you need it. Keep your focus on the vision of restoring your marriage, so that you can get back in touch with the strengths you have and the values you hold dear. You have the handouts. Look over your Vocabulary List of Feelings (see page 197), and we'll be ready to start using the processing skill at our next session. Now let's take a break for today! You've earned it!"

Navigating Oceans of Emotions

Sharon entered Dr. Brightman's office, seated herself, and got out her water bottle and notepad, ready to get down to business. Stephen approached his end of the couch, stretched his back and shoulders, and sank down into a stiff posture, wearing a look of resignation on his face. Dr. Brightman smiled as she greeted them. "How has your week been?"

"Well," Sharon said, "I'm going to explode if I try to hold it in. So, yes, I yelled at him a lot and said, 'How could you do this? You have destroyed our marriage and ruined our family!' The boys are feeling the brunt of this, with all the tension in the house. I've had to take a lot of timeouts and go for long walks," Sharon sighed.

"When I come back in, I've calmed down a little, so I try to talk with Stephen again and tell him how I feel. At first, he listens, but then, like you said, he starts making excuses and defending himself. Of course, that makes me even angrier, so we're in a standoff. We barely speak to each other at home, so that we don't disturb the boys even more," she continued. "I have a lot of bad days. I'm struggling, and I'm sure he doesn't like to hear this."

"Well, all your attacks and blame sure don't help anything!" he growled.

"It sounds like you both badly need the processing skill we're going to practice today. I see you brought your handout for feelings and your Processing Skill handouts. I'll try to make it easier by guiding you through the steps. We're going to start with Sharon. Stephen, you will have the opportunity to process during another session, okay? Are we all on the same page?"

"I hope so," Stephen replied. "I'm pretty anxious about this. It really puts the spotlight on me!"

"It really does. Okay, Sharon, have you decided on a particular incident that you'd like to process?"

"Yes, I'd like to process the time when I discovered the shocking text messages between Stephen and Holly that were an undeniable revelation of his involvement with her. Sharon I was shaking with fear and could hardly catch my breath my heart was racing so violently. I tried to scream, but nothing came out; It was such a shock. My whole world came apart in that one moment. I was devastated, angry, and hurt. I felt so betrayed, and I wondered how long this had been going on. I could only think of all the lies he must have told me. I was completely overwhelmed."

"Now, turn to Stephen, and say that."

"Stephen, what you did left me feeling shocked, devastated, and broken, like I was coming apart at the seams and completely terrified," Sharon sobbed.

"That was huge, wasn't it? Stephen, what did you hear Sharon just say?" Dr. Brightman asked.

"Sharon, I heard you say how devastated, angry and hurt you were and how it rocked your world," Stephen repeated.

"Well, it's worse than you could ever imagine. I don't know if I'll ever be the same," Sharon sobbed, as tears spilled down her cheeks.

"Stephen, do you understand why she would be that overwhelmed? Can you validate her feelings?"

"I know that I hurt you terribly, Sharon. I can't imagine you not being devastated. It had to be heartbreaking," Stephen's voice was barely above a whisper.

"That's exactly right, Stephen," Sharon choked on her tears. "You really broke my heart. I trusted you."

"Stephen," Dr. Brightman prompted, "how would you feel if Sharon had betrayed you and cheated on you? Do you think you would feel the same way?"

"Sharon, if you had done that to me, it would be my worst nightmare come true. I don't know how I could live with that." Stephen was shaken at his own response.

"Maybe now you can grasp just a little of what I've been through," Sharon gasped. "Looks like you practically wrecked your marriage, Stephen," Dr. Brightman observed. "Can you apologize for what you did?"

"I am so sorry, Sharon. I must have lost my mind. But I do love you and I want to stay married to you." Stephen tried to look into Sharon's eyes, though she turned her head away.

"Yeah," Sharon acknowledged, looking downward. "I wish I could believe you."

Dr. Brightman turned back to Stephen. "Ask Sharon what she needs from you right now."

"What do you need from me right now, Sharon?"

"I need to know that you're not having anything to do with Holly anymore. And I need you to show me that you are still attracted to me."

"As I've told you, I've cut everything off with Holly," Stephen reiterated. "I do love you, Sharon, and I'll be glad to demonstrate how attractive I find you!" he said in a low voice, as he leaned over and gave her a hug.

The doctor was pleased. "This was a great start, you two. You did a great job! We'll be following this process several times in our next sessions to allow you to get the poison out, so to speak. You look like you want to say something, Sharon."

"For the first time, I feel like Stephen is beginning to realize how badly he hurt me. It does feel better to think that he can listen, relate to what I've been going through, and take responsibility for the mess we're in, rather than always trying to shut me down."

"I'm not gonna quit now, Sharon. And if this is what it takes, I will do it." Stephen reached over to squeeze her hand.

"Well, I can't think of a better note on which to end this session, can you?" Dr. Brightman asked with a slight smile.

The couple smiled back. Dr. Brightman silently wondered if she'd just seen a glint of hope in their eyes. As they made their next appointment, she wished them well on their way out.

The Other Side of the Coin

A week later, Dr. Brightman welcomed Stephen and Sharon back to her office. As usual, she asked them for an update on their progress since their last session.

"Well, things have settled down a little. But we're still not bringing up 'the issue,'" Sharon related. "I don't think I can control my emotions enough yet to follow the directions without your help. I know I'll just explode, like I usually do. So, again, I'm taking long walks and short shopping trips as timeouts."

"You're doing the right thing, Sharon. It sounds like you're in touch with what you need to do. And, practice makes perfect! So, let's take another shot at processing those emotions," Dr. Brightman suggested.

"Well, okay," Sharon began, reaching for her bottle of water and smiling, "but I think I really need something a little stronger than this."

"Sorry about that, Sharon, but I can't help you there! I don't have any liquid fortitude to offer you," the doctor joked.

"Alright then. I guess I'll just brave it on my own," Sharon chided. Then she took a deep breath and whispered, "I'd like to process my feelings when Stephen lied to me saying his turnaround flight had been rescheduled. I presume he was right here in town, in a hotel with Holly the entire time. It was only later that I found out the truth, when I saw the local Hilton Hotel on his credit card bill for the exact date his flight was rescheduled." Sharon groaned while giving Stephen the evil-eye.

"That had to be a mind-blower," the doctor responded. "What a shock! Tell Stephen what that did to you."

"Right—here goes," Sharon glared at Stephen. "It felt like my heart stopped. I couldn't get my breath. First, I felt tremendous dread and fear. My mind raced, and my whole body shook. Then I was swallowed up in anger when I realized you lied to me about that, Stephen, and I believed you. I felt so stupid!"

"What are you hearing, Stephen?" Dr. Brightman prompted.

"Sharon, I guess you must have been in a panic," Stephen said woodenly, as he twisted his fingers around each other.

"I just crumbled," Sharon remembered.

"Can you understand that, Stephen?"

"Well, I never thought about it from that point of view. Obviously, it would have been so shocking that you felt it down to your bones," Stephen mumbled. "Nobody likes to be lied to, especially about something so unimaginable," Stephen continued sheepishly, staring at the floor, and overwhelmed with guilt.

Dr. Brightman interjected, "Stephen, would you please look at Sharon when you're talking to her?"

"Well, okay, I will. But it's really hard for me to do that right now. I've been hiding behind this mask, and it feels like it is being ripped off."

"I'm sure it does. What if she told you a lie like that, and you discovered it? What would that be like for you?"

"It would destroy me to find out Sharon lied about something so shocking. I can't even put words to what I'd feel," Stephen stammered helplessly. "I'm sure I'd be in a rage, though."

"Believe me, Stephen," Sharon said. "You'd be absolutely livid!"

"It's hard for me to listen to this. One lie just led to another," Stephen sighed in exasperation.

"Can you ask her what she needs to feel better?"

"Sure. What can I do right now?" Stephen was clearly relieved to shift the focus of the conversation.

"I need for you to know how much this hurt and how much it's destroyed my trust and my self-esteem. It's been a nightmare, and I need you to let me talk about it. You've got to quit trying to shut me down."

"Okay, but it's really hard to listen when you scream and yell at me, Sharon," Stephen whispered softly. "I just want us to get through this and not keep going over and over it. I don't want to look back."

"Stephen, you may need to listen to this several times before Sharon can get over the damage it caused," Dr. Brightman encouraged. "But sooner or later, she will feel better, if you keep talking it out with her. And Sharon, please use **'I feel'** statements rather than attacking and yelling at Stephen. That will make it easier for him to listen. I know this doesn't change what happened, but doesn't it help when he listens and acknowledges the pain he's caused you?"

"Yes. I need for him to do that. I need to know Stephen cares and is truly sorry for what he did." Sharon carefully dabbed at her tears, trying not to further smudge her makeup.

The doctor nodded. "Alright. We've completed a couple of processing rounds now. How are you holding up, Stephen? What has this been like for you?"

"Painful. It is draining, exhausting. I feel a lot of shame and guilt, and yes, tons of regret! I wish it had never happened. But if you think this helps Sharon, I'll keep doing it," Stephen added.

"Take a few moments to catch your breath," Dr. Brightman recommended. "Then, why don't we try processing what you just told me? I heard you mention several feelings just then."

"Sure. I guess I'm game," Stephen said reluctantly.

"I heard you say you felt very guilty and are left with a lot of shame and regrets about what you did. You also said you felt exhausted and drained. Is that right? Can you tell that to Sharon?"

"Those feelings churn in my gut all the time, Sharon," Stephen began. "I'm really angry at myself, when I look back."

"Okay, Sharon," Dr. Brightman asked, "Can you reflect back what you heard?"

"Well, you said you're full of shame and guilt. You said you feel a lot of regret and are even angry at yourself," Sharon parroted, rolling her eyes.

"Is that what you wanted Sharon to hear from you, Stephen?"

"Well, no, not really. What's with the eye rolling, Sharon? That tells me you don't really believe me. You're just mocking me."

"Stephen, tell Sharon what you felt again."

"Whether you believe me or not, Sharon, I feel a lot of guilt, regret, shame, and anger at myself," Stephen repeated. "That is all rolled up in my head all the time like a big ball of trash."

"Sharon, what did you hear this time?"

"Okay, Stephen. I'm hearing how guilty you are and how much you regret what you did. And you're angry with yourself for pulling a trick like this. Is that right?"

"Yeah. That's more like it," Stephen acknowledged.

"Sharon, does it make sense that he'd feel that way?"

"Darn right! He should feel that way because of what he did. You think you feel shame, Stephen? I'd like to give you a dose of the shame you put on me!" Sharon rebuked.

"Whoa, Sharon, this is Stephen's time to process. You've got to keep your focus on him right now. Could you rephrase that, please? Try to stay on course here and validate his feelings."

"I know I'm supposed to, but this is hard. I hear that Stephen feels that way, and I can understand why," Sharon admitted flatly. "When you do something that hurts someone so badly, there would be a lot of guilt and shame attached to things you want to hide." "Now, can you imagine yourself in his shoes? If you got caught up in an affair like he did, what would you feel when he found out?"

"Maybe I ought to give you a dose of what it'd be like, Stephen, if I had cheated on you!"

"Timeout! Timeout! That's not going in the right direction," the doctor scolded. "Can we please stay on track? I know it's hard to stay focused on the process—that's the hardest part of this. It takes discipline."

"Fine! Stephen, I know you would be completely devastated if I cheated on you. I'm sure I'd be beating myself up, wondering how I'd ever get out of this. I'm sure I'd be haunted with regret and remorse," Sharon concluded, her brows furrowed with concern. "I am sorry we have to go through all of this. What do you need from me, Stephen?"

"It is good to know that you are at least trying to understand that I've been suffering through all this too, even though it is my fault. What I need to know is that you'll try to forgive me," Stephen implored.

"I don't know, but I hope that I can eventually," Sharon gave him a sideways glance. "But I don't think things will ever be the same."

"What do you say to that, Stephen?" Dr. Brightman prompted.

"Just keep telling me that we can get through this and that you'll give me another chance. Sometimes I feel like giving up."

"I feel that way too, sometimes. I never thought we would get caught up in something like this. It's been hard on the boys too, seeing us go through this."

"Kudos to you both! You're getting an understanding of the impact this is having. You're knocking out a little chunk of this pain every time you process like this. Sharon, when you're having a bad day, tell Stephen you need to sit down with him and process what's going on with you. Let him know you need for him to listen. See if you can use this pattern of communication at home. The more you practice, the easier it will be. Just keep trying," encouraged Dr. Brightman. "We can process again in our next session. I know it was tough today. For now, you both need a little breather. Maybe it's time for another shared good time with no mention of any of this then, okay?"

"Yeah, I'm ready to relax and enjoy a good meal at our favorite Mexican restaurant. Let's do it!" Stephen urged.

"I think I may need a margarita or two," Sharon smiled.

Dr. Brightman rose to walk the Sloans to the door. She said a silent prayer for them as they scheduled their next appointment. As they left her office, she noted that their moods and their body language seemed somewhat better.

In the Foxhole

The following week Stephen and Sharon perched themselves at their established positions in Dr. Brightman's office.

Dr. Brightman was intent on getting the next lesson across. "Listen carefully, because although you don't hear much about this, it is the strong glue for holding a relationship together. It's one of the most important keys in relationships: **emotional intimacy**. It's based on our normal emotional needs. You know, we're all born with certain dependency needs. As children, of course, we need to be taken care of physically, as well as emotionally. As adults, we're no longer physically dependent upon others to meet our basic survival needs, such as food, clothing, and shelter. But we never outgrow our emotional needs. What do I mean by that? We all have needs for emotional support, encouragement, approval, appreciation, nurturing, comfort, reassurance, affection, and attention. These are among the basic emotional needs we never outgrow. These are what we depend upon our loved ones to fulfill. I've never heard of anyone who doesn't want those things, even though they may not be aware of it."

"You know, I thought Sharon just needed me to fix whatever was upsetting her or solve her problem. I always felt good when I could do that," Stephen said emphatically.

"Yeah, sometimes I do want a solution to whatever's bothering me," Sharon agreed. "I get what Dr. Brightman is saying, but I feel like you don't, Stephen. You know, sometimes all I really want is for you to 'baby' me a little!"

"What? You mean, that's what you've been looking for all this time? I thought you'd be impressed when I was 'Johnny on the Spot,' ready to fix whatever was wrong!" Stephen replied in wonder.

"Well, I know it sounds strange, but, yeah, that's it! I guess sometimes I just want some emotional pampering. But, Dr. Brightman, how do I get that?"

"First, you have to be open and honest about your feelings by sharing your struggles and what's bothering you. He won't know your unique experience unless you tell him. He should lean toward you with words of compassion to comfort, reassure, and support you. Call it emotional pampering, if you must. That's **emotional intimacy.**

"It's about giving and receiving emotional comfort to and from each other and acting as each other's best friend. Best friends take each other's side and have each other's back. They say, 'I'm with you and for you.' They look to each other for compassion, understanding, and reassurance. Does this sound too syrupy?"

"Well, I've always been a fan of maple syrup on my pancakes, so pour it on, Doctor!" Stephen joked.

"I think I like this flavor of syrup. It's got a different taste than I'm used to, for sure!" Sharon laughed, too.

"Good, then I'll continue. We all know how to comfort a hurting or frightened child by making him or her feel safe, secure, and loved. Yet, somehow, we lack the ability to provide that same level of comfort and support for each other. In our culture, we are conditioned to believe we don't need this kind of emotional nurturing, but the fact is, we all need reassurance, comfort, and encouragement. When you understand this, you will see numerous opportunities to emotionally connect with each other. Couples who don't make this connection drift apart. They report feeling lonely, empty, and isolated. They end up turning away from each other, rather than toward each another. A word of wisdom here: remember to offer your emotional support before rushing in with solutions. Solutions can come later. You want to serve as a buffer to stress for each other—like aspirin is to a headache," Dr. Brightman paused and took a breath, then continued. "Emotional intimacy is probably the strongest bond in human nature. It's the foundation of any meaningful relationship. Amazing, isn't it? People don't want to detach from someone who has the ability to meet these emotional needs because it forms such a strong bond."

"Why don't we ever hear about this?" Stephen said. "It's just common sense, but no one ever talks about it."

"Yeah! This is like the world's best kept secret!" Sharon chimed in. "This is what I've always wanted from Stephen, but didn't realize it until you explained it just now. That's been missing in our marriage forever!"

"I never thought about it that way. We never really knew that was missing!" Stephen added, his voice rising. "Wow! Is that a bombshell, or what? At least it is for me."

Dr. Brightman smiled, "Let's take a few moments to think about some times you can recall where you needed emotional support. We're not trying to assess blame here. We just want to take a snapshot of what each of you experienced at a moment in the past when you really could have used some understanding and compassion. Stephen, let's start with you this time. Can you think of a time when you needed Sharon's support and understanding?"

"Let me think for a minute," Stephen paused momentarily. "What comes to mind is when the pilot's union was planning a strike against the airline. We were getting a lot of backlash from management and administration. They were putting up resistance to our demands. Sharon had difficulty understanding the position I was in when the union asked us to picket. She didn't see the point of our efforts. I remember her saying, 'That's silly; you know how they are. You shouldn't be surprised. They're greedy. They're in it to make a profit. You're just wasting your time.'

"I certainly felt disrespected, misunderstood, and as though she didn't appreciate me. She was unsupportive. She just didn't comprehend the stress I felt. Fortunately, administration finally came back to the table with enough concessions that we were able to work things out. But the whole situation was just so stressful! I know Sharon wasn't in the position to do anything about the outcome, but it really would have made me feel better to have her in my corner throughout the ordeal. I actually felt like she was on management's side, rather than on mine. She seemed insensitive to the distress the entire situation caused me."

"Thank you, Stephen. Sharon, do you remember that?"

"Sure, I remember. I was in the middle of a big decorating project and felt that you were just whining a lot, Stephen. But I really didn't think it was going to amount to much. Management always plays these games, and picketing seemed pointless. But I guess you're right—I wasn't very sympathetic or reassuring. Looking back, it's obvious I missed the point. I thought I was just trying to help you sort things out. Sorry 'bout that, Stephen!"

"Can you see that Stephen felt unsupported?" Dr. Brightman asked. "Your support and compassion would have buffered a lot of the stress that Stephen was feeling. How about you? Do you remember a time when you wished Stephen had backed you up?"

"Yeah, I'm pretty sure Stephen already knows what I'm going to say. It would be when my father had a bad fall. My mom was so worried and upset that she asked me to fly out and help her with Dad. I knew she needed me. Dad's not the best patient, and he has diabetes. But when I told Stephen, I was shocked by his reaction. He said that my dad wasn't in imminent danger, and he had good doctors. He thought I was over-reacting. It never occurred to him that what I really needed from him was his support, understanding, and reassurance. He really wasn't very compassionate, not even kind," Sharon explained with a heavy sigh.

"Stephen, what's it like hearing this? Do you understand how alone Sharon felt?"

"I was preoccupied with getting my rating in a new aircraft. It threw me off balance to suddenly have this on my plate. Sharon, I was worried about your dad too, but I guess it didn't come across that way. I guess I was insensitive. I was so preoccupied with my own concerns that I didn't realize what you were going through. Yes, I knew you'd mention that, and I'm sorry you had to face that alone."

"Sharon, what was it like for you just now, hearing this?"

"Well, I'm glad you realize how upsetting that was for me, Stephen. You're right. I felt alone and completely abandoned by you. And that made all of it harder to bear. I wanted to be a support to Mom and Dad, and you just shot me down. I could have used your understanding and reassurance," she added, taking a deep breath.

"You can imagine what a difference it would have made if you had turned toward each other with emotional support," Dr. Brightman explained. "It wouldn't have changed the situation you were in, but it would have made the road a lot easier, and you wouldn't have felt so alienated and alone. When you connect with one another with compassion and tenderness, it creates a positive feedback loop—building both of you up and strengthening your relationship.

"Think about how you can bring more emotional intimacy into your relationship. I'm going to give you some handouts that will help with this. You can give me feedback in our next session. I'm encouraged by your participation!" complimented Dr. Brightman.

Getting Back in Touch: The Icing on the Cake

"Hi, Dr. Brightman, how are you?" Stephen asked, as he led Sharon by the hand into the office.

"I'm doing great! How are you two doing today?"

"We're doing pretty well," Sharon answered.

"Wonderful! Let's hear about your week. Did you remember to give one another more emotional support?"

"Oddly enough, those lessons in emotional support arrived just in time to help us through a tough spot," Sharon responded. "Travis, our youngest, dislocated his knee Saturday evening in the soccer tournament. We spent most of Saturday night in the emergency room."

"Oh, no! That's painful. How is he?"

"He'll be fine in a few weeks, but now he's on crutches and all wrapped up. To answer your question, he's out for the rest of the season" Stephen looked somber. "What we learned last week was very helpful in getting us through the whole ordeal.

"Stephen was on his way back from Chicago when it happened, so I had to call him from the hospital. I was so distraught. Travis was in a lot of pain. Stephen was so comforting and reassuring. His usual response would have been, 'Calm down, Sharon. You need to be strong for Travis.' Normally Stephen would be giving me orders. But Stephen came straight to the ER from the airport. I was so relieved. He was so supportive and instead of grilling me, he complimented me for my handling of the situation."

"Yeah, we were pretty lucky," Stephen added. "Nothing was broken, but he'll be restricted for a while and he's going to hate that!"

"So, you can see how stressful that situation could have been without emotional support. With that support from each other, you were better able to reassure Travis."

"That's right. At first, we weren't sure of the extent of his injury. He was in pain and fighting the doctors," Sharon recalled.

The counselor nodded, "And you remembered to reach out and lean toward each other. Let's take some time to look at another bonus of the intimacy factor. As you become more emotionally intimate, you will be naturally drawn to be more physically affectionate, because emotional intimacy and physical intimacy are closely linked. As you feel more emotionally connected you will experience a desire for more physical connection, as well. When you have loving and caring feelings toward one another, it sets the stage for those feelings to be expressed physically. Does that make sense?"

"It definitely does." Sharon turned toward Stephen, "I know when I feel connected to you; I want to be close to you physically. And when I don't, it's just the opposite."

"And, I like to know that you care about me, think about me, and appreciate me, too. That sets my desire for you in motion."

"That's how one thing leads to another, and that's another example of a positive feedback loop," their counselor pointed out. "We usually think of physical intimacy as meaning only sexual intimacy. But physical intimacy includes all kinds of a loving, caring touch. When you feel close to someone, you approach them with hugs or a pat on the back, or even a kiss on the cheek. Hugs, handholding, a goodbye kiss, sitting arm-in-arm, back rubs, snuggling, and cuddling are all forms of physical intimacy. Do you see this progression?"

Sharon and Stephen nodded their understanding as Dr. Brightman continued. "The most fulfilling and satisfying sexual intimacy results from feelings of close emotional connection. Most married people want to make love, not just have sex, right? Making love means being in touch emotionally."

"After Holly was out of the picture, I felt like I had to prove myself to Stephen sexually, so I became more sexually assertive, to prove I was as desirable as she was," Sharon answered. "I had crazy thoughts that he would be comparing me to her. I just wanted to show him how wrong he had been about her—and about me. I'm still struggling with a lot of mixed feelings."

"Sharon, explain what you mean about having mixed feelings," The doctor urged.

"It's like I'm caught between two opposing forces," Sharon began. "Now, I'm glad I don't have all those lurid details of their disgusting relationship, but I can imagine what he's done with her. And my imagination sometimes runs away with me, which makes me feel like I have to prove myself sexually. Then, on the other the hand, I want to avoid him because of what he's done. He poisoned our sex life!" She choked back raw emotion. "So, that's where I am right now—not in a good place about that."

"You mean you're 'torn?'"

"Yes, unfortunately. I just wish I never had to go through any of this. It's so unfair! I have so many doubts—not just about him but about myself."

"That's why I hope you will move slowly, until you feel more comfortable and secure. Timing is so important! I'm going to explain more about what I mean in just a moment. Are you on board with this, Stephen?"

"I guess so, but I'll be glad when we move past this. I feel like I've done everything I'm supposed to, and I think Sharon knows at this point that I'm committed to our marriage. But patience is not necessarily a virtue I possess," Stephen groaned.

"Let me give you a few suggestions. This should be a natural process and can't be rushed. Sharon, you don't have to prove yourself or put pressure on yourself. Stephen, try just holding hands or giving a hug or back rub with no other expectations. Remember that you're trying to create emotional closeness here, not just a physical act. You will know when the time is right to move forward. Meanwhile, continue having shared good times, including romantic dinners to set the stage. As you feel more closely connected, you will want the physical connection, as well. How about some feedback on this?"

"It all makes sense," Stephen spoke out. "Sharon, now that all this has come out, I really want you to know that you don't have to prove yourself to me. What I really want is for our sex life to be what we make it, and not a reaction to anything else."

"That might take a miracle, Stephen. And thank you, Dr. Brightman, for not putting a high-pressure deadline on this. That would just push me further back right now. I really like what you said about the emotional connection."

"You both want that, don't you?"

"Absolutely," Stephen answered. "Of course, I want to feel closer to Sharon, and I want her to feel close to me. I don't want our sex life to be just a performance."

"The main thing to remember about this is to follow your natural inclinations. What feels comfortable and what doesn't will tell you where to go. Be sure to express your feelings, and respond with understanding," Dr. Brightman emphasized. "Just take your time. It will work out. Now, how do you feel about coming in for a follow-up in two weeks? Does that sound alright?"

"I'm okay with that," Sharon responded.

"Sure," Stephen added with a grin, "I'm hoping we'll have some progress to report when we come back. See you then, Doc."

Rising from the Ashes

Dr. Brightman was unable to suppress her smile when Stephen and Sharon next entered her office arm in arm. For the first time they sat down together on the couch.

"Welcome back," she greeted. "Let's get caught up. I hope you two have had time to experiment with some of the things we discussed at our last session."

"Actually, Stephen, you have been showing more encouragement and support," Sharon reported. "It shows you're making the effort."

"I've discovered that I'm a big fan of the 'positive feedback loop,'" Stephen shared enthusiastically. "I'm looking forward to seeing how much more positive things can get," Stephen waggled his eyebrows at Sharon.

"I saw that!" she joked.

"As far as the physical goes," Sharon began, "Stephen, it is reassuring and nice when you hug me and put your arm around me when we're walking or sitting together. It's nice that you want to hold my hand, too. I feel like you're starting to court me, all over again.

"He is beginning to notice little things I like, Dr. Brightman. He brought home a bottle of my favorite wine the other day, even though it's expensive. He said he just wanted to let me know he had been thinking of me. He's also picked up a few cards for me and added some personal notes that have really touched me."

"Don't forget how much better I am at listening to you now, too," Stephen reminded her.

"That's actually true! The other night, we talked for hours. That's the first time that's happened in a very long time."

"I never liked getting into conversations before, because it had this pattern of turning into a litany of complaints," Stephen admitted. "But I enjoy it when we spend time together and have discussions without going off on tangents."

"Dr. Brightman observed. "Yes, it's so funny that people think that guys don't like to talk. But they certainly do whenever they have a friendly environment and don't feel on the defensive." "Yeah, I want Sharon to be my best friend. You know, a friend with benefits!" he chuckled, nudging Sharon. She returned his smile warmly.

"Well, I can certainly see a difference in you two!" Dr. Brightman noted. "Even though this has been a traumatic experience that has shaken your marriage to its foundation, you are turning things around by working through this together. It has taken a lot of courage. Some couples would have given up."

"I'm so glad we've had your help, Dr. Brightman. I couldn't imagine how this would ever have worked out, but I'm feeling much more hopeful," Stephen replied soberly.

"I'm afraid the outlook for our marriage would have been pretty dim," Sharon agreed, "But things are looking better."

"Well, you're doing just what you need to do. If it's working, keep it going. If you keep doing what you're doing, you'll keep getting what you're getting. How does that sound?"

"So far, so good," Stephen quipped.

"I want to give you a quick review: Of course, you'll want to continue your **shared good times**. That should be easy," the doctor summed up. "The more you have fun and enjoy each other, the more you will want to spend time together, and reinforce the bond between you."

"This has turned out to be our easiest step," Philip noted. "We really missed out on that. We just have to keep up the routine of setting aside some time together. I'm enjoying courting Sharon all over again."

"Yeah, we really sort of lost track of each other."

"And of course, you need to keep the **boundaries** you've set. You need to be able to state where you stand—your personal comfort zones—and don't expect to be mind-readers. Those boundaries with Holly are set in stone. They should definitely not change. But, you can always renegotiate other boundaries, if you both agree to it. And you have your handouts to refer to any time you need them."

Sharon's mood shifted and she turned to Stephen. "Are you still holding the boundaries we set on Holly? I still need your reassurance about that, you know."

Stephen responded wearily. "You ask me that all the time. Yes, I'm holding the line." "Sharon may need to hear that more often than you think, so be aware of that, Dr. Brightman reminded. "Now, let's move on with the review. Can you tell me what you need to do when emotional tension escalates?"

"I know!" Sharon snapped. "When I'm hurt and angry, you need to shut up and listen."

"Well, that's a heck of a way to put it!"

"Are you getting a little tense right now?" Dr. Brightman inquired. "By now, you should be able to recognize the signals when you need to take time to sit down and process through your feelings. Using the **REVEAL process** you learned."

"Umm...yeah. I guess we just missed a few of those signals," Sharon confessed. "But you never did listen before, Stephen, and I wonder if you'll remember what Dr. Brightman's taught us."

"Why borrow trouble? Let me be the one to worry about that."

"You have your handouts to keep you on track," the doctor reminded. "Go over them, so you'll be ready when things hit the fan. Unless you want **negative feedback loops**, remember that **processing skills** help calm things down pretty quickly. If you need to take a **timeout**, do it! Return and go through the process like we practiced."

"At first, I thought that was kind of cheesy," Stephen admitted. "But it does seem to work, so hopefully, we will get better at this. The hard part for me is being able to stay in control and listen. I want to fight back!" "This will be quite a change, if we can manage it," Sharon added. "I used to feel like I was just a problem that you needed to solve. I felt like you just wanted to drown me out."

Stephen agreed. "Well, you would think that. But we're making progress."

"Remember, Sharon: sauce for the goose is sauce for the gander," the counselor noted. "That means you'll have to be on your toes when Stephen is upset, too. Try to move into a processing mode before things escalate, or you will find yourselves in the negative feedback loop again."

"I'll be working on that one. It's really hard at times to have much compassion for his feelings when he gets so intense."

Dr. Brightman smiled. "I understand that, but here's the good news: You now have a skill you can use to change that. I notice the two of you are creating a new vision for your marriage. And why focus on the past, when the future looks so much brighter? This has been a long and difficult road, but you have met the challenge. So, I'm going to release you. Of course, you are always welcome to come back for tune-ups or check-ups at any time."

"I like the way you put that, Dr. Brightman," Sharon noted and Stephen agreed.

"You know a lot more now than you did when we started. Build on that!" Dr. Brightman encouraged

After sharing a group high five, Sharon and Stephen left feeling hopeful.

The Warrens

CHAPTER 3

Hitting Rock Bottom

Watch out! Depression is contagious! Sick people make healthy people sick!

Before we move on to the last couple, let's talk about **Osmotic Depression**. It is a silent destroyer of many marriages. There are volumes of information focused on those diagnosed with depression. Its symptoms, treatment, medication, etc., are discussed in dozens of books. But not much attention has been given to the people who live with or are married to the depressed. They suffer in silence and often feel invisible.

This chapter illustrates what it's like for the forgotten and ignored—those who live lives of quiet desperation with their depressed partners. Their story deserves to be told. Depression has become epidemic in the United States. It is a leading cause of disability. But those who are diagnosed with depression aren't the only ones who suffer. Their symptoms have an extremely negative and debilitating effect on those around them.

In my practice as a marriage and family therapist, I recognize that clinical depression and its untreated symptoms are a significant cause of marital discord and failure. Negativity, irritability, anger, mood swings, and pessimism create a toxic environment. Loved ones are left with no choice but to live in constant frustration and stress, or decide to leave. But most don't have a clue about the struggle they personally deal with. They are confounded and confused by the interactions and observations they experience, having no realization they are dealing with the dysfunctional behavior of a clinically depressed person. Therefore, any effort to engage the depressed person through normal or rational behavior is exhausting or even futile. It can lead to a depressed state in the otherwise healthy individual.

Relationships with depressed people are strained by erratic moods, irrational outbursts, and oppositional defiance. Nothing pleases them—at least for long. They are compelled to always complain about something or someone. The depressive has a mindset that makes it difficult for the couple to form necessary goals, make decisions, and resolve conflict. What is often decided or determined one day may be vigorously opposed the next. Arguments and factions create friction and cripple the couples' ability to collaborate on important issues. Confusion blocks effective communication and the pursuit of activities as well as intimacy, as the depressed person retreats into his or her own dark world. Partners are left to figure out what went wrong, and when there is no obvious explanation, they often blame themselves.

So, the partner doubles and redoubles efforts to keep the peace and fix the problem. What they don't realize is that two different views of reality exist: the reality of the partner and the reality of the depressed individual. Those who are depressed are often at odds with present reality. They see themselves as victims, and vehemently challenge any oppositional view. It is common for them to cling to irrational beliefs and opinions without the ability to explain their perception. This is an intolerable dilemma for the partner who is entangled in such a world, he or she may begin to doubt their sanity. An utterly helpless and hopeless feeling of despair settles in. This is the formula for **osmotic depression**, which is absorbed from the depressed environment in which they live.

Lacking any reasonable explanation, many partners develop maladaptive coping and defense mechanisms, or behavior that is counterproductive, becoming depressed themselves. However, some manage to escape by recognizing that they are helpless to change the status quo and begin independently pursuing activities and relationships they enjoy while others hit a threshold, can no longer tolerate the chaos, and exit their marriage.

It is crucial for partners and family members to recognize the signs and symptoms of depression and encourage the symptomatic individual to seek help. This is usually met with resistance, but at some point, the clinically depressed person may realize the depth of his or her condition and yield to pleas to seek help before their relationships are irreparably damaged. Most types of depression are treatable. There are many antidepressant medications that have been proven to be effective. Therapy is also beneficial in teaching new coping mechanisms and relationship skills. Research confirms that this combination of medication and therapy produces the most beneficial results.

What to look for:

1) Signs of depression in yourself or your partner;
2) Watch for erratic behavior patterns;
3) Notice how depression harms your relationship;
4) Notice how the depressed person affects you;
5) Notice the use of emotional language to address needs.

Now, meet the Warrens.

Catalysts for Change

Claire Warren was a 35-year-old married woman who, despite her accomplished legal education and professional status, found herself in a deep, personal slump. A nose-to-the-grindstone workaholic, she had managed to avoid taking inventory of her personal circumstances. Recently, however, Claire had become acutely aware of the innumerable concessions she had made to the dreams and ideals she once held for herself.

Looking in the mirror annoyed her. She only saw a compromised version of herself in the reflection. When she was younger, Claire had taken the time to carefully craft her professional image with tailored business dresses and suits, stylishly coiffed hair, and perfectly applied makeup. Now, she wore what she jokingly called her "uniform"—a matching blazer and slacks with a high-necked print blouse, accessorized with simple black pumps and matching silver necklace and ear studs. Her dark brown hair was cropped short so that she didn't have to spend much time on it, and was lightly sprinkled with flecks of silver that was matched by her jewelry. She kept her nails trimmed short and unpolished. The only makeup she took the time to apply these days was a quick sweep of mascara and lip gloss before dashing out the door to the law office. It had all become too much of a chore.

She was usually the first to arrive at the office each day and the last to leave, working under three partners, handling cases they didn't want, and supervising the paralegals. But lately, even getting to the office was a struggle. She had to drag herself out of bed every morning, lacking the motivation she once had. She was bored and disinterested and couldn't see her career going anywhere.

Claire probably could have continued to explain away her change in demeanor indefinitely, had she not recently attended her college class reunion. While there, she ran into Sandra, a former sorority sister. The two reminisced about their old plans and dreams while sharing a bottle of wine. Sandra had achieved her goal of becoming a juvenile court judge, and she regaled Claire with stories that described the sense of reward and fulfillment she received from guiding young people toward a more productive path.

When she and Sandra had studied family law in college, Claire recalled expressing a goal to have her own practice, specializing in women with family issues. She'd felt driven to assist women in all aspects of their lives. Her biggest passion, though, was to legally advocate for those who had been abused or sexually assaulted. Looking at the path her law career had taken though, Claire felt disappointed in herself. She had no fire in her belly anymore—just a nagging sense of duty to perform her job—no sense of satisfaction or progress.

Sandra shared the histories of some of the youth she had helped over the years, along with tales of their antics and adventures. But Claire found herself with no practice of her own, no prospects of starting one, and no stories to tell. She surprised herself by spilling out her frustrations and disappointments to her old friend, and Sandra seemed uncomfortable and somewhat eager to end their conversation. Claire felt awkward. She wanted to explain to Sandra that she wasn't jealous of Sandra's accomplishments; she was just disappointed in herself.

After returning home, Claire dug out her college yearbook to study old photos. She was astonished at how she'd changed, and was shocked to discover how much of her "self" and her ideals she had lost. She wondered how she had ended up in this position. Something had gone horribly wrong, but she couldn't identify a specific time or event that had turned her life in this direction. She had somehow slowly drifted off course without noticing.

"It's high time you took stock of yourself and figured out how you got here," Claire told her reflection in the mirror. "You've got to get a grip, and dig yourself out of this rut! I don't like what you're doing, and I'm not happy with the person you've turned out to be. For Pete's sake, you need to face the fact that you may even have to be the sole bread-winner soon, if Philip loses his job. You'd better make some changes before you completely lose it!"

So, Claire found herself contacting Brighter Day Counseling services and making an appointment with Dr. Carla Brightman. The next week, she entered the waiting room a little late and sat down nervously. She switched chairs twice as she waited, and was relieved when the counselor entered the room and greeted her.

"Claire, it's so nice to meet you. Please come in and get comfy," Dr. Brightman welcomed.

Claire apologized. "I'm so sorry to be late. My directions to your office weren't good. I went too far down the road and had to turn around and go back through all the lights." "Don't worry about it," the doctor soothed. "These things happen. Is this the first time you've been to see a counselor?"

"Yes, it is. I have a lot on my mind—a lot going on and a lot to figure out." Claire's feelings just flowed out of her in a torrent. "My husband is on disciplinary probation at work and is in danger of losing his job. That situation has me worried that I may soon be our family's sole breadwinner. Believe me, Doctor, this hasn't been easy for me to face! Philip is forty-three, and we all know that men in that age bracket with lots of experience can lose out to young college graduates who don't require big salaries. Also, the realization that I've held back for years on advancing my own career has shocked me into reality. I went to a college class reunion last week. That experience caused me to come face-to-face with some things about myself that I don't like. I've decided I need to talk to someone about it. I don't know what's wrong exactly, but I know I need to make some changes, and I hope that you can help me untangle all of this."

Dr. Brightman smiled. "Well, that's why I'm here, Claire. So, what is it you don't like about yourself?"

"I'm really confused. I don't know if I'm having a mid-life crisis, or what I'm dealing with, exactly, but I know I'm not myself, or at least not who I thought I would be. I feel like a failure as a wife and as a person. I don't have the marriage or the career I've always wanted. Nothing I do pleases my husband. I feel stuck, and I don't see any way out of this. I don't have any energy or motivation whatsoever, and that's not like me, Dr. Brightman. I used to be confident and hopeful and passionate, but now I just beat myself up every day. I feel like I've let myself down, and I don't know why or how this happened. I don't even like myself anymore, and I don't see any hope for a better future," Claire added plaintively.

"That's a big burden to carry around. You're obviously in a lot of turmoil. No wonder you feel so tired all the time."

"I'm overwhelmed! Everything is such an effort." The words continued streaming out of Claire. She seemed unable to stop them. "I can't express how I feel to Philip. He just explodes and tells me I don't know what I'm talking about. He yells, 'Get a grip!' So, I just shut down. My anxiety has gone through the roof. I'm constantly walking on eggshells, never knowing when he's going to erupt and criticize me. I notice I've gotten so forgetful that I can't stay focused on anything for very long, and it's causing problems at the law office. I feel like I'm just going through the motions, paralyzed. It's like I can't do anything right." She finally stopped long enough to grab a tissue, catch her breath and dab her eyes.

"You're feeling helpless and can't see any way out. Is that true?"

"That's it exactly."

"You've got several things going on at once here," the doctor explained. "I think it's important to take some time to go over each of these to make sure I have a clear understanding of your situation. Tell me a little more about your husband: your background as a couple, how you met, how long you've been married."

"Of course. When Philip and I married a little over five years ago, I had just finished working my way through law school and had passed my bar exam. I wanted to get a small business administration loan and start a women's advocacy law firm. Philip talked me into postponing the whole idea. He said that starting a new practice would mean waiting years before turning a profit, and he didn't want us to start our marriage in debt. He thought I should get a paid position so that I could help with the bills. Philip had been married before, and was left with a lot of debt. He said he never wanted anyone to put him in that position again.

"So, I gave up the idea for the time being. I've regretted it ever since. Anyway, I took a ground floor position at the firm where I'm still working. I've discussed leaving there to start my own practice with Philip several times since then, but my timing has always been off—according to him. First, it was because we were trying to start a family, and he didn't think we'd be happy juggling the priorities of a new prac-tice with a new baby—which he really wasn't enthusiastic about anyway.

"After we learned we couldn't have children, I decided to refocus on launching my practice, but again Philip shot me down. I've given into him time after time, but Philip still isn't happy. It seems that nothing really makes him happy anymore. He's always complaining about something. So, I just sort of gave up on any plans for opening my own practice. I've dug my heels in at work and just stopped thinking about what I wanted. It doesn't seem to matter anyway. It just wears me down," Claire sighed.

"That's very frustrating! No wonder you're so drained. It seems that every time you've wanted to move forward, you've been blocked."

"Exactly! And, you know, I have just as much difficulty recognizing the person my husband has become as I do myself. I had such high hopes for us when we first married. Philip was so charming and supportive and encouraging while we were dating. He showered me with attention and affection, and I thought I'd found my soul mate—the man of my dreams," Claire shifted uncomfortably in her seat before continuing.

"After Philip graduated from college, he married and began working toward an MBA, but he gave up after several unsuccessful attempts to pass the entrance exam. To pay off his student loans, he was forced to take a job he considered beneath him, working as an assistant manager of a large bank. Since then, he hasn't gotten much further in his career. When we met, I thought he was a wonderful guy who had just had a streak of bad luck after going through a bad divorce. I felt like I could get him out of his rut, and help him make a fresh start. I guess I had a pretty idealized image of the situation. Now he has become bitter toward his boss, the management, and even the bank customers, but he makes no attempt to find better options or to improve himself. I've tried to encourage and support him, but he dismisses my help; criticizing my ideas and suggestions, telling me that I'm not exactly a success myself." Claire rubbed her palms against the arms of her chair, but then she stopped herself.

"It doesn't really make sense, does it?" Dr. Brightman inquired. "He complains a lot about his situation, but doesn't really take any action to try to change it. Some people just want to complain about their problems. They don't do anything about them. It makes everyone around them feel as miserable as they do."

"I guess that's one way to put it, Doctor. But according to Philip, everything's my fault, not his. "You mentioned that he was on disciplinary probation at the bank.. What's that about?"

"Philip was written up at work a couple of months ago because he had taken out a bank loan to cover his credit card debt. When he got behind on payments, the bank called the note. Here he is, back in debt, where he swore he never wanted to be again. On top of that, Philip was called on the carpet again last week over an unrelated incident. His unprofessional behavior with a VIP client caused him to be placed on disciplinary probation. He lost his temper with the client and was so rude in the way he handled her that she reported him to his boss. And apparently this wasn't the first time this kind of thing has happened. So, Philip's boss required him to go to counseling immediately, or lose his job."

"So, that does put you in the shaky position of possibly becoming the sole provider. That's another heavy burden."

"Everything's in a whirl. So much is going on, and I don't see how we can ever figure it all out. I've even considered filing for divorce," Claire confessed, dropping her eyes and her head, looking defeated.

"You definitely have a lot on your plate, and Philip's behavior is only making it worse," Dr. Brightman empathized.

"Once I've started talking to you about it, it's seems like I can't stop! I've really never spoken to anyone about this, so I didn't even realize how much I've held in. I'm kind of shocked myself!"

"Actually, you may not realize it, but what you've described sounds like Philip may be depressed."

"Oh, my gosh! That's exactly what Philip's doctor said. He just got his evaluation from the psychiatrist, and the doctor diagnosed him with something called pervasive depressive disorder. He told me the doctor prescribed an antidepressant and recommended a counselor. Since compliance is required for him to get off probation, Philip really has no choice but to follow through. Even though he despises his job and his boss, he feels he can't leave the bank. He says that if and when he leaves, it will be on his own terms, not someone else's," Claire added, checking Dr. Brightman's face to see if she was following.

"I see. Well, this is an interesting situation. This could be a teachable moment for Philip." Dr. Brightman said knowingly. "Claire, there are literally millions of people in this country struggling with depression. This situation is very common today. I have some handouts that I'm going to give you to help you understand more about it." Dr. Brightman reached into a folder on her desk and passed the handouts to Claire.

"Thank you. Do you think this might explain Philip's behavior? Is there really a medication that will help?"

"Yes, this type of depression is usually very treatable. Sometimes, medications have to be changed to find the right one. But when the right prescription and dosage is established, anti-depressants are effective in rebalancing moods, and counseling helps the individual develop better coping mechanisms. If Philip will follow through, you should see some changes. And when his mood improves, it will lift a burden from you. Meanwhile, you might want to delay considering any drastic actions such as divorce. We can talk more about this and how it's affecting you at our next session. Can you come again next week at this time?"

"Sure. This may explain what's going on with Philip, but I still wonder about what's going on with *me*. I just know I'm not the same anymore," Claire lamented with a sigh. "I'll look over these handouts before I come back."

Catching a Bad Case of What's Going Around

Claire arrived for her next appointment flushed and out of breath, but ready to dive right into her session. "Wow, Dr. Brightman, you were right on the mark! I've carefully read these handouts, and it's remarkable how Philip exhibits so many of those symptoms."

"I figured that you would recognize some of his behavior. It seems he may have been depressed for quite a while. From what you told me last week, it sounds like it is a chronic condition."

"Well, I felt better just being able to talk to you about what's going on. Last week, when I started talking, I couldn't stop. I've been keeping a lid on this for months! It helps just knowing there's some explanation for his behavior. It's been good to put a label on it. I never really knew what depression really was. I just thought Philip was being obnoxious and acting weird," Claire mused. "And I am surprised to learn that so many people are also affected. I really don't think anyone realizes this."

The doctor nodded. "People are bewildered when they can't explain the odd behavioral changes they see. They don't know what they are dealing with, and usually think it's something that they caused. I heard you say that you felt it was your fault you couldn't make Philip happy. Claire, it's important that you know it's not your fault that Philip is so unhappy and behaves the way he does. In fact, just the opposite is true. He projects his misery and anger onto you. Philip's depression has actually brought you down!"

Dr. Brightman emphasized this. "Remember what I said last week? I am concerned that Philip's behavior is dramatically affecting you. Do you realize how many dysfunctional attitudes and patterns of behavior you've picked up in order to live with Philip's depression?"

"I think I get it. You mean I've had to change myself in order to accommodate Philip. Are you saying you think that's what I'm dealing with?" Claire asked, looking confounded.

"I'm saying that you really have had no choice but to adjust to his moods and twist yourself like a pretzel to continue living with him. I can see that you've compromised your own needs to handle Philip's behavior, and this has harmed you emotionally. His criticism and treatment has obviously damaged your self-esteem and threatened your well-being. It looks like you have come to believe his critical judgments.

"It's common for those who are depressed to shift blame for their negative and hostile moods onto someone else. When you live with someone who is depressed, you are vulnerable to becoming depressed yourself. You tend to internalize that depression. What I'm saying is it's depressing to live with someone who's depressed! I refer to this as **Osmotic Depression,** because as with osmosis, you absorb the depressing environment," the doctor said gently.

"What? That can't be right. I've never thought of myself as being depressed. I know I'm struggling, but do you really think it's actually depression? I certainly don't act the way Philip does!" Claire challenged.

"It's a different kind of depression than Philip's, which his doctor apparently feels is most likely a chemical imbalance. He probably has some family members who have been depressed, because depression tends to run in families. What you have is different: your environment is the source of your depression, so this is a type of depression connected to your situation. As I mentioned earlier, you have what I call osmotic depression. I hope this makes sense."

"Yes, but it's freaking me out! It never occurred to me I might be so affected by Philip that I was depressed, as well. I kept thinking that my unhappiness and dissatisfaction with my life was my on failures and never a result of my relationship with Philip."

"While you're pondering this, I'm going to give you another handout that explains this a bit more. You can look over this information." Dr. Brightman handed Claire a crisply printed sheet of paper. Claire accepted the page and, as she scanned it slowly, her jaw dropped.

After a few moments of Claire's stunned silence, Dr. Brightman spoke. "Looking at the symptoms of depression, you can see a pervasive and persistent pattern of negative and pessimistic moods. This is much more than when someone occasionally has a bad mood.. It's more like staying in a bad mood and infecting others with it."

"Like a virus or bacteria?" Claire asked. "It's contagious like that? I never thought of a mood as being contagious. But, now that you've explained it, I guess in some way it is."

"Can you make the connection between Philip's depression and your downward spiral?"

"I'm going to try. Here goes," Claire began. "Anything can set him off. He has these rage attacks and starts yelling and screaming and blaming me for anything and everything. So, I blame myself and wonder how I could be so stupid. He says everything I do is wrong! He criticizes my friends, and he can't stand my mother. I have great friends, and I love my mother. It really hurts. I'm sick of hearing about it and resent him for it. He does it to insult me—" Claire paused to reach for a tissue.

"So, you can see how he's affecting you," the counselor pointed out.

"Yes, I am angry and resentful. But isn't it normal to get ticked off when someone treats you that way?"

"Of course, it is. Anything else?"

"Even when things are going well, he can't enjoy it, and that ruins things for everyone else, particularly me. When friends invite us out, Philip drinks too much and becomes critical of whatever political news is on his radar. I'm too embarrassed to accept invitations anymore, so I usually just pretend we already have plans. On weekends, all he wants to do is have a couple of drinks and sleep. Sometimes he'll sleep for ten hours or more. He stays shut up in our darkened bedroom most of the weekend, like he's hibernating, so I feel lonely a lot." "Sounds like this has just about ruined your social life, as well."

"It definitely has! You know, Dr. Brightman, even when things are going well, he imagines obstacles and problems. I've never seen anyone constantly borrow trouble the way he does. I feel defeated before I ever get started with anything, because he argues with me and shoots me down. It's just not worth it to try to pursue anything. All of this makes me feel so hopeless and that things will never change."

"Claire, you're doing so well at connecting his behavior to your own feelings and responses. Do you see how debilitating this is to you? I'm sure it must wear you down."

"It is, and it does. But I'm seeing even more, now that I've opened this can of worms. I also end up taking responsibility for his feelings, and just agreeing with whatever he says to keep the peace. But whether I agree with him or not, he still wants to argue. It's crazy! I find myself crying at the drop of a hat. I don't like feeling this weak and helpless," Claire sobbed. "I just can't win."

"You can see that you've been living in a toxic environment. So, I'm glad Philip is seeking help now, and hopefully your home life will start to reflect his improvement. It's important, however, that we discuss this and make a plan. I'd like to take a few minutes to do that right now."

"Sure. What do you have in mind?" Claire asked curiously.

"In addition to meeting with me, I would like for you to think about attending a group I lead on Thursday nights here at the office. It's for those who, like you, have been living with a person who is clinically depressed. I think it will help you to hear what others are going through, and I believe you will be able to relate. When people share their experiences with others, they don't feel so alone. It becomes reassuring to realize that you aren't the only one going through something like this. It helps you to feel compassion for yourself and gives you support and encouragement. It also keeps you grounded by reinforcing the thought that what you're dealing with is not caused by you and you can't fix it." Then Dr. Brightman handed her a brochure on the support group.

"Wow! I think that's a great idea! I feel relieved just knowing that there are other people going through the same things."

"Well, there are enough people living with clinically depressed family members to start groups like this everywhere. You know, as a marriage and family therapist, I recognize that depression and its symptoms are a significant cause of marital discord and failure. Unfortunately, most people living with or married to someone who is clinically depressed have no idea what they are dealing with. It's very confusing; they expect a normal mindset and rational behavior, but they're dealing with a depressed person who is often irrational and dysfunctional."

"I guess you just keep trying to make sense out of nonsense and it gets nowhere," Claire added.

"Exactly! In our group, one of the things we will discuss is how to function in a dysfunctional environment. Would you be able to join us Thursdays evenings from 6:30–8:00?"

"Well, I think it would be good for me, so I'll see you Thursday night, Doctor," Claire gathered her things and turned to leave.

In the Same Boat

Claire arrived early next Thursday evening for the group session. She was visibly nervous as she watched the others come in and take their seats. There were four other women and three men joining the group.

Dr. Brightman started things off. "Hi, everybody! I want to welcome you to the recovery group. I'm glad you're here. Please get comfortable. I want to give you information about how we conduct our meetings. Most importantly, I want to make it very clear that everything we discuss here is absolutely confidential, and no personal information is ever to leave this room. Each of you will have a time to share, and I will do my best to keep the conversation flowing in a productive direction.

"The goal of our group is to encourage and support each other by sharing our common situations and respective ups and downs. In this manner, each of us can see how the others are struggling with the same type of circumstances. I will intermittently offer guidance and direction, but I want to allow you to freely express your feelings. This is to be a safe place for that. I'll be talking to you about **processing skills**, **boundaries**, and **self-care** for example. And, I'm going to empower you to **be your own best friend**." Dr. Brightman paused to see if the group had any questions on what she had just explained. At that point, she asked everyone to go around the room and introduce themselves. Afterwards, she addressed the group again.

"Now, I'm going to share some basic information about depression. I want to reassure each of you that you neither caused the depression being experienced by your loved ones, nor can you fix it. According to research, there are often physiological imbalances in the chemistry of the brain that affect the moods of individuals suffering from depression. Depression can sometimes be triggered by a crisis, but chemical imbalance can also disrupt the individual's stability. However, the type of depression each of you is experiencing is a result of living with a depressed person. We call this **Osmotic Depression,** depression through osmosis, since you have absorbed the dysfunctional patterns and moods you've been living with."

The doctor then began to outline the group's objectives. In order to help group members shift focus away from their dysfunctional partners, she encouraged each one to sort out and seek their own interests and activities in order to form a more individual lifestyle. They were encouraged to seek activities that gave them pleasure, which would reinforce their own self-esteem and identity. Dr. Brightman told them that it was a time to take the initiative and follow up on plans or interests they had put off or ignored. It was a time to get in touch with themselves and their own unique likes and dislikes. She reminded them that focusing on the depressed person and his or her needs would only drag them further into frustration and despair as their efforts to rally the depressed person continued to fail.

Claire realized this was what had happened to her. She had focused on Philip and tried so hard to please him, and deflect the anger he projected onto her. She felt exhausted just thinking about it. *How did I get so drawn into his chaos?* she wondered.

Dr. Brightman gave each person in the group a handout to help them identify personal interests and goals. She followed up by telling them she would outline tools for setting appropriate boundaries and teach them how to befriend themselves. She closed the meeting and invited the group to linger a few minutes for coffee and conversation.

The Best Friend in the Mirror

"Hi, Claire, come on in. I'm interested to know what you thought about the group session the other night. I'm so glad you were able to join us."

"I'm really glad I came, even though it seemed kind of awkward at first. I want to continue coming, it's just that I'm not used to sharing my dirty laundry with others. It feels like I'm doing something wrong, like I'm betraying Philip or something. I wonder what people would think of me if I really expressed some of my deepest feelings? I hope I wouldn't be judged too harshly. So, you can see I have some reservations," Claire confessed.

"Most people who have participated in groups like this have told me they feel the same way at the beginning," Dr. Brightman reassured her. "After a while, I think you'll be more comfortable, because you will see that others are experiencing situations very similar to your own. It's stepping out of your comfort zone for sure, but you will benefit," Dr. Brightman reassured her.

"I know: No pain, no gain, right?"

"You got it! Now, what's going on at home?"

"Everything seems a little quieter than usual right now—maybe too quiet. Philip has been sullen lately, rather than critical and complaining. I think both of us are realizing how trapped we've felt. I'm now aware more than ever how much Philip's depression affects me. Knowing others in the group must be struggling has helped me realize that it's normal to react the way I have. But I feel stuck. I don't know what I'm supposed to do next," Claire admitted, looking perplexed.

"See how you've lost touch with yourself? You've got to find yourself again. You need to think about the person you've always wanted to be, Claire. We need to work to reclaim your life, your dreams, and your identity. You have literally been disconnected from the internal hardwiring that made you 'Claire' and have rewired yourself to handle Philip's moods.

"Today I have an exercise that I want us to work on together. I'm going to help you write a letter to yourself. This exercise kind of turns you inside-out emotionally, but it will help you understand how to become 'your own best friend,' by speaking encouraging and empowering messages to yourself. For example, do you have a sister or a close friend? Someone you really trust?"

"Sure. I've been close to my friend Marian since we were in junior high. She and I have been through more than a few trials together. Marian has always been there when things have gotten tough."

"Then, let me ask you this: If Marian were going through what you're going through with Philip, what would you want to tell her? You would certainly be on her side, wouldn't you?"

"No matter what!" Sharon declared.

As Dr. Brightman offered Claire handouts, she continued speaking, "So, **you need to be able to do that for yourself**. You need to be able to act in your own best interests—as long as others aren't harmed. You have to treat yourself as you would treat your best friend. By that, I mean making self-care a priority. This means stopping all self-criticism and self-blame, because you are just filling yourself with negative emotions. When you find yourself doing that, STOP! Don't engage in negative self-talk. When you notice you're saying something negative about yourself, refuse to stay there. Instead, turn it into a positive message. Think of this as driving on the highway. When you notice you've taken a wrong turn, simply turn the car around and drive in the right direction. Get it? It's simple, but not easy.

"You must also be able to forgive yourself. Everyone makes mistakes, and you don't want to hold yourself in bondage. It's common knowledge that we need to forgive others, but we don't even realize that we also need to forgive ourselves. Otherwise, we stay stuck with regrets.

Treating yourself like a best friend is a corrective measure that will help get out of the habit of condemning yourself. I suggest you frequently refer to the handouts I've given you and familiarize yourself with them for next week. I'm going to review these with you then."

Using this information, Dr. Brightman asked Claire to begin writing a letter to herself, as though she were writing to her best friend. She then allowed Claire time to put her thoughts on paper. Claire swiftly began writing, never looking up.

When she finished, Dr. Brightman spoke. "I'd like you to read your letter aloud, so that you can literally hear your own voice, giving yourself hope and encouragement. Begin whenever you're ready, okay?"

Claire cleared her throat, lifted her paper, and began to read in a soft, but expressive voice.

Dear Claire,

I'm sorry you've had to live with so much heartache and pain. I know when you married Philip, you wanted a loving and caring relationship with him, but your hopes and dreams have been dashed. I know how discouraging it is that your marriage hangs by a thread, and you really don't know how it got there. You've tried so hard to make things work and keep the peace. You've had to keep so much to yourself, while inside you cried silent tears. You've had no one to share your heartache with because you thought you deserved the treatment you were getting, and you felt so ashamed. You never deserved it. You should have been treated with respect and love as Philip's wife.

He's the one who should be ashamed—not you. Even though Philip has told you that you're a drag and no fun, the truth is that you enjoy other people, and they enjoy you. I'm going to make sure that you get out and pursue the things you like to do. Even though Philip told you that you let yourself go, the truth is you are attractive, and I'm going to make sure that you stay that way. Claire, you are also smart, and I believe in you. You've worked so hard, and I promise, I'll help you get where you want to go. It's time we cleared up these old beliefs you've been carrying around in your head. Those were his beliefs about you—not yours—and you don't have to accept them anymore. I want to help you find yourself and reconnect with your hopes and dreams to enjoy a brighter future—with or without Philip.

I will not allow Philip or anyone else to keep you from your goals and dreams. You have my permission to open a law practice if you want, and I will cheer you on and help you get there. Your days of putting Philip's demands ahead of your own needs are over. You are my top priority today, and every day, from now on. I want you to be the best you can be!

Your BFF (Best Friend Forever),

Claire

Claire's sobs had nearly drowned her words as she read the letter.

Dr. Brightman allowed Claire to stay in the moment. "It's okay to cry. Crying is a healthy way to express the sadness and grief you've felt. Weep freely! You've obviously been grieving the marriage and life that you've lost for a long time. Your letter expresses your compassion for yourself and your loss. But it also is a witness for the life you yearn for and the joy awaiting you."

At last, Claire's sobs let up, and she tried to speak. "I-I-um…I guess I just never realized"how much of myself I'd lost! It's so horribly sad! For years and years of my life, I have had absolutely no mercy on myself. This letter has helped me see how cruel I've been to myself. I blamed myself for everything and beat myself up constantly. No wonder I've been in such a terrible place. I would never treat anyone I care about the way I've treated myself," Clair sobbed softly again.

After she finished, she folded the letter and placed it in her purse. "I want to like myself more." I know I need to stop beating myself up. I'm going to have to read this over and over, so I can convince myself."

Dr. Brightman nodded. "You're doing just what you need to do to get through this. This is not going to be an overnight change, but sooner or later, you'll begin to believe in yourself again. Yes, please take the time to read your letter again and again. Start saying those things to yourself regularly. Correct yourself when you say or think belittling thoughts. Don't follow that negative train of thought any longer! **What others say to us has a definite impact, but what we say to ourselves impacts us even more!** Let's keep moving forward with this plan. I'm hoping you can join us again this week for the group meeting," Dr. Brightman said as she walked Claire to the door, "but if not, I'll see you next week."

Crossing the Threshold

Claire seated herself in Dr. Brightman's office the next Tuesday.

"Hi, Claire—I want you to know I really liked your best friend letter last week. It was an excellent expression of what you have been experiencing. How do you feel about it now?"

"I'm proud of myself for being able to write down the things I need and want, without feeling guilty." Claire smiled, "It was sort of a revelation to know that it's okay to feel good about myself and to act in my own best interests. Before, I thought saying those things would make me full of pride. It seemed selfish. Like you described, the letter writing kind of feels like turning yourself inside-out. However, when I read it, I do feel a little more empowered.

"I think as I get more in touch with myself, I won't get so defensive with Philip. There were a few times this past week he tried to pick a fight with me, but I just told him that I wasn't going to participate. Since the weather was so nice, I went for a few long walks. I practiced taking timeouts, like you taught us in the last group meeting. When I would get back, he seemed to have gotten the message and didn't pick the argument back up," Clair exclaimed. "It felt good being able to take control of what I will or will not listen to, for a change! I realize I can't stop Philip's verbal assaults, **but I can stop allowing him to influence me so much**. And, I can leave him standing there by himself, with no one to hear his criticism—THAT feels powerful!"

"Good for you! You're certainly sending yourself the right message."

"But Doctor, I want to talk about something else today. Lately, I find myself snapping at Philip all the time. Then I try to drown my anger with a couple of glasses of wine at night."

"That's a defensive mechanism you're using to swallow your anger towards Philip. Anger makes you uncomfortable, so you just suppress it."

"I'm sure that's right, but inside I'm furious. It's scary for me to even admit that. I'm afraid if I start to let this boiling anger out, I won't know where or when to stop! It's overwhelming to consider," Claire blurted out, "but I feel like I want to give Philip a dose of his own medicine!"

"You certainly have permission to vent your anger here and in the group setting. It's normal to be angry after how you've been treated and what you've been through. It would be abnormal if you weren't angry."

"Sometimes I absolutely hate him. I want to tell him off so badly and tell him how selfish and abusive he's been. I want him to see the hurt he's caused me. I want him to know what it's like to feel the way I do. He needs to be the one who feels guilty—instead of me—and full of remorse. Why should he get away with his behavior?"

"I hear your anger, Claire. Do you see how deeply it has affected you? Now, I'm going to give you an assignment. I want you to write an anger letter to Philip—but not give it to him. It's for therapeutic purposes only. This will provide you with a productive way to get your anger out. You may not know it yet, but anger is energy, and you can feel it inside. You feel the adrenaline, your blood pressure goes up, your heart rate increases, you start breathing more rapidly, and you become sweaty. If you don't release this anger in a productive way, it will come out sooner or later, usually with consequences. If you stuff down too much anger, it will affect your health. You can see that when you project your anger back onto yourself, you load yourself with more emotional distress. This is called **retrograde anger**," Dr. Brightman explained. "You're putting all that hurt and frustration back inside when you blame yourself for Philip's problems."

"Oh, yeah! I can see that I've done that, thinking I was responsible for Philip's unhappiness and misery. I thought, if only I had done this, or I hadn't done that, he would be happy. Or I thought that if I had just let him rant about anything and everything, he would get over it. I felt like I should know what to do," Claire added, pointing to her head.

"So, you can see where a lot of your anger went: back on yourself. That's why I want you to write an anger letter to Philip. You need to redirect your anger to the appropriate source. You'll put words to your anger by writing that letter. This will help you get in touch with how you actually feel and express it without hurting anyone."

"You mean I can write anything I want?"

"Why not? As long as it's about your anger towards Philip."

"How do I get started?"

"I want you to jot down some bullet points of things he does that make you angry. This will be the format for your letter. Your greeting might read, 'To Philip, regarding my anger.' Then start out by filling in the phrase, 'I'm angry because _____. I'm angry because _____. I'm angry because _____. And keep doing this until you've listed the things that make you angry. Do you think you can do this?" Dr. Brightman asked cautiously.

"It will be my pleasure," Claire sneered. "Finally, I get to tell him off!"

"I want to ask you something else. Would you be willing to bring your anger letter with you to group with you on Thursday evening and read it to the others? This would be a powerful tool in helping you, as well as the group. I'm sure you realize that everyone else in the group is probably just as angry as you. I'll be there to help you, if you need it."

"It would be kind of embarrassing, but if you think it will benefit the group, I'll do it," Claire responded thoughtfully.

"Wonderful! I'll be looking forward to hearing your letter. Don't worry about making it sound perfect. Just pour out your feelings on the page," instructed Dr. Brightman. "I appreciate your cooperation with this. Can you plan to meet with me fifteen minutes early before group, just to check in?"

"Okay. Yes, I'll feel better about this if I can take a few minutes to talk with you before we start the meeting."

"Good. See you Thursday night!" Dr. Brightman waved as Claire left.

Leading by Example

The two women met that Thursday prior to the meeting.

"Good evening, Claire. How did it go with writing your anger letter?"

Claire knitted her brows, "Well, it was really different, but it helped me to get in touch with my anger. Once I got started, the words just poured out, until I finally had to stop myself. I think I could have gone on and on."

"I hope this didn't stress you out too much!"

"Not really. It felt good to put into words what I've been feeling for so long. It made me realize how much hurt and anger I've been living with. Here it is," Claire handed over the letter.

Dr. Brightman paused to quickly look over Claire's letter. "This is exactly what needed to come out! Are you still willing to read this to the group?"

"Sure! Now I feel better about doing this." The two of them walked into the meeting room and took their seats.

Dr. Brightman welcomed the group, "Well, I see we have a full house tonight. Glad to see everyone made it back! I want to check in with everyone to see where you are. Chris, will you be the first?" Everyone listened as each member followed with a brief update.

"Chris mentioned how much anger he had toward his wife, Jeannie. I think this must have struck a chord in many of you. We're going to talk about anger tonight. In my private session with Claire this week, she mentioned her anger toward Philip. She was worried that she was about to blow a gasket. I instructed her to write down her anger in a letter to Philip. She wasn't supposed to give this letter to him. Instead, I invited her to read it tonight to the group. Claire agreed, so I'd like for her to proceed with that now. How 'bout it, Claire? Are you still okay with doing that?"

"Sure. Here goes," Claire unfolded her letter, cleared her throat, took a deep breath, and began with a heavy sigh.

To Philip, regarding my anger:

For years, you've raged at me, belittled me, blamed me, and insulted me, until I'm worn out. You've had no right to treat me that way. That was abusive, and I don't deserve it. You are ruining our marriage and destroying my sanity. I'm angry with you because:

You blame me for your problems, your foul moods, and your mistakes.

You complain so much that I can't enjoy anything anymore.

You tell me that I am incompetent and incapable.

You say one thing and do another.

You turn every conversation into a battle.

You sleep for hours and hours. It's like you're dead to the world, and I feel ignored.

You clutter up the house with your messes, and don't care if that makes more work for me.

You make excuses for everything, and you think you're never wrong. It's always someone else's fault—usually mine.

I'm anxious all the time because I have to walk on eggshells around you. Your behavior makes me crazy.

You yell at me and threaten me if I don't do what you want.

You criticize my family and friends and never shut up about it.

You're self-absorbed; you've never once looked at the damage you've done to me.

I'm finally beginning to see how your problems have affected me and I won't tolerate it any longer. I will not allow you to treat me this way. I'm better than that. If I have to leave, I will. You are a drain. This is not a marriage—it's a joke that's not funny!

Regretfully, Claire

Claire's hands shook as she lowered the letter. Tears streamed down her cheeks, and she reached for the tissues. "It's really terrible to get in touch with how he's affected me, Doctor. I don't know why I didn't see it before. I feel so stupid. I guess I've taught Philip over the years that he can treat me this way and get away with it," she sobbed, as Martha, the woman next to her, patted her hand to comfort her.

"Now you're turning your anger in on yourself, Claire." Chris interjected. "I know what that's like—I do it, too!"

"I'm sure most of you have done the same thing," the counselor pointed out. You've turned your anger back on yourself when you don't know what else to do with it."

A resounding "Amen" arose spontaneously from the group.

"That was an incredible letter, Claire," Dr. Brightman continued. "I know it hurt to read that, but I'm so proud of you! You are facing a reality that is so painful."

"I hate what this has done to me. I just hate it!" Claire choked on the words. "I don't think I can ever go back to that kind of insulting treatment."

"You don't have to make any decisions right now. When you're able to get this pain out, you will be in a better place to determine what you want to do. It's never a good thing to make a life-changing decision when you're in such a vulnerable, emotional state."

"But I've got to get past this," Claire moaned.

"I believe you will. You're doing what you need to do. Let's keep going, shall we?" Dr. Brightman turned to the class, "Claire's letter is an example of what I would like each one of you to do. As I did with Claire, I'm going to give you some directions that will help you get started."

The members of the group agreed that they wanted to write their own letters, so Dr. Brightman spent the rest of the meeting telling them about different types of anger. "People think that if they don't admit their angry feelings, they aren't angry. They just repress it. I've heard people say they aren't angry, even when the cruelest and most abusive things have been done to them. Chris just shared with us an example of **retrograde anger**, the type of anger that you project back onto yourself and then feel guilty. These are examples of '**internalized anger**,' meaning the anger stays trapped inside. Be aware that there are complications of physical distress and illness from this type of anger. There is also a type of '**externalized anger**,' such as anger displaced onto an innocent party. Perhaps, when the boss yells at the husband, and then he yells at his wife, and the wife then yells at the kids, and the kid kicks the dog; the anger just trickles down to the most vulnerable party. Haven't you all seen this? This is a type of **displaced anger**."

The group nodded their heads in unison.

"Why does this happen?"

"It's really a cowardly way to express anger. When the consequences are high, a person will address anger toward a less threatening target, where the consequences are lower. In other words, when they think they can get away with it."

"That sounds like bullying," Martha interjected.

"That's exactly what it is," the counselor concurred. "These are all destructive and unproductive ways to deal with anger. Now, a word of warning: If you fear someone is beginning to react violently or becomes violent, then you need to call 911! Don't be afraid to pick up the phone and call for help if you feel physically threatened."

Martha looked startled. "I never realized that there were so many ways to deal with anger. It all sounds destructive to me!"

"Unresolved anger *is* destructive, Martha. I would also add that some people abuse alcohol or other substances. This is called 'self-medicating.' As people seek to medicate their anger, they are at additional risk of developing addictions. So, you can see why I want all of you to write an anger letter," Dr. Brightman summarized. "It's actually healthier to release anger in this non-destructive and productive manner."

"Well, I'll go for that!" Ken joked enthusiastically. "Does anybody have paper on sale this week? I'm going to need a lot of it!"

"Yeah," added Patsy. "Maybe we can all go in together! I'm going to need a whole pack of ballpoint pens."

"Sounds like you're all enthusiastic about this assignment." With that, the doctor handed out some additional information to the group for them to study.

"Before I dismiss our meeting this evening, I want to briefly go over the material I just gave you. These handouts cover a few important do's and don'ts. Don't engage in any provocative arguments when that other person starts to berate and bully you. Take a **timeout**, go to another part of the house, and close the door. Or leave and take a walk or a drive. I hope this doesn't happen, but if you are blocked or threatened, express your fears and explain that if the person continues to rage and frighten you, you will call 911. Are you with me on this?"

"Yes, I sure am!" Claire asserted.

"But writing an anger letter seems very strange for me," Patsy commented. "I've always thought of anger as being a harmful emotion that needed to be controlled and suppressed. Won't this make me sound like a mean person, Dr. Brightman? I grew up hearing my parents say, 'If you can't say something nice, don't say anything at all.'".

"Anger is a survival emotion, Patsy," Dr. Brightman explained. "Babies are born expressing anger when their needs go unmet. But I hear your concern. Anger, in itself, is neither bad nor good—it depends upon how you use it; how you express it. It's like fire. You can use it to warm yourself and cook a meal, or you can use it to destroy property or harm someone. Writing about the impact of anger doesn't hurt anyone, and it will help you to release it productively."

"I never thought about it that way," Patsy replied.

As they left, Chris playfully mentioned to the group that Claire would be the only one with no homework that week. And then he added, "Just come in ready to get your ears burned!" as they filed out the door. The others in the group all turned to Claire to thank her for her courage in sharing her anger letter with them.

Preparing to Cross the Great Divide

When Claire came back into Dr. Brightman's office the following week, she was eager to report her progress, and the counselor said, "You did such a fantastic job Thursday night, sharing your letter with the group! It really seemed to make a difference to everyone."

"I'm really looking forward to hearing everyone else's letters." Claire enthused. "It's such a relief to have gotten mine over with."

"Well, thanks again, Claire. Have you been able to continue reading your 'Best Friend Letter' to yourself, as well? As you keep reading that letter to yourself, you're forming new thinking patterns, so it's important to continue what you're doing," Dr. Brightman encouraged with a broad smile, as Claire nodded. "And now I want to ask you how things are going with Philip."

"I'm glad you asked. He's been seeing his counselor regularly for over a month now. At first, he was very angry about having to go, and resisted. Of course, he had no choice if he wanted to keep his job at the bank. As you recall, he had also been referred to a psychiatrist who prescribed an antidepressant, which I believe he's taking on a regular basis. And, his counseling sessions are supposed to help him develop better coping mechanisms. I can tell that he's less angry and critical, and that's a welcome relief," Claire sighed. "So, I believe he is serious about getting better."

"I'm so glad to hear this! The antidepressant will help elevate his mood and modify his depression. It sounds like the counseling is helping as well."

"There has definitely been less tension and strife in our home, but there is still a lot of distance between us. It seems like we've sort of declared an uneasy truce for the time being," Claire opined. "It's a relief not to have so much contention, but our relationship is still broken. Even though things are better, I don't want to live like this forever. So, what are we supposed to do now?"

"This may be a good time for you and Philip to come in together and work to reconnect and rebuild. The depression you've both experienced has taken a huge toll on your marriage, hasn't it? We've got to take steps to put this marriage back together. How do you feel about that?"

"That actually makes me a little nervous. I'll probably get some resistance from Philip over the idea. It will certainly be awkward for both of us, sitting in the same room together discussing all we've been through. Based on our history, we'll probably end up in a big argument. We just see things so differently! I don't think he even realizes the impact his depression has had on our relationship."

"He probably doesn't, Claire. But let me reassure you that I will keep the sessions focused on solutions and the skills you both need. I believe this is the best step for now. Think about it."

"Well—nothing ventured, nothing gained, I suppose. I'm willing to move on," Claire announced bravely.

"So, you will talk to Philip about coming in with you for some joint sessions?"

"I'll do my best. I have no idea what to anticipate from him, but I know we can't leave things as they are. I'll give you a call later this week after I've talked with him and see if we can set something up. I feel better having the 'Best Friend letter' to give me confidence—no more time lost doubting and questioning myself."

Claire called Dr. Brightman several days later to report that Philip had reluctantly agreed to come in for a joint session. "But he said, 'Oh, no! Not another counselor; won't we ever get a life again without having to go to counseling?'"

Philip assumed that he would be targeted as the "identified problem." Claire managed to convince him, however, that couples' counseling was necessary if they wanted to restore their marriage. She related that Dr. Brightman was concerned that their routine would settle back into the same rut if they didn't acquire new skills. Although they'd both felt some relief from the depression, they needed to reconnect with one another and get new ideas to help them improve their communication and resolve their lingering conflicts. Philip had finally agreed to participate in the joint sessions as long as he was assured that he would not be the object of blame and criticism. So, Claire called Dr. Brightman to arrange their meeting.

"Claire, I'm so glad you called. Fill me in. How are things going between you and Philip?" the counselor prompted.

"Good to talk to you again, Doctor. Philip and I have discussed everything and agree that we do, for sure, need to come in together."

"Excellent. How about Tuesday after work? Say 5:00 p.m.?"

"I'll check with Philip, but put us down, for now. If he has a conflict, I'll call back and reschedule," Claire hung up and marked her calendar.

Fingers Crossed

Claire led Philip into Dr. Brightman's waiting area that Tuesday. They were both anxious, but Philip seemed particularly reticent and tense. "Claire—what have you gotten me into here?" "I think I'm just about 'therapied out.' Are you sure this lady knows what she's doing?" "Well, she sure has helped me! You know, my nerves were on edge, too, the first time I met her, but she just has this way of making you feel like everything's going to work out. I'm a little jittery myself this afternoon—just because I want things to go well for us. Let's just give this a shot, okay?" Claire encouraged, as she squeezed Philip's hand. She realized the future of their marriage was at stake.

Dr. Brightman entered the waiting area and welcomed them. "Philip, It's so nice to meet you. Thanks for coming today." As they seated themselves, she asked, "How do you feel about this appointment? I imagine you're pretty uncomfortable at the moment. Most people are, so don't worry about it. I want you both to know that this is a safe environment for you, and I will do everything I can to ensure that our sessions are as productive as possible. We're not here to point fingers or assign blame, but to put our heads together and figure out what you both want in your relationship. I'm just here to serve as a guide during this process."

Philip gave Claire a sidelong glance, "I've been in counseling, so it doesn't really bother me, but I hate the idea of having to rehash our problems. It brings up so many bad feelings, and I'm sure I'm going to be labeled the bad guy." "I assure you I won't be taking sides, Philip." Dr. Brightman promised. "That would certainly be a therapeutic error. The 'good guy/bad guy' roles result from an interactional pattern between the two of you, which creates a negative feedback loop because misunderstandings and anger set you against one another. So, you see, in reality, you both are contributing to the problem, in one way or another, and we need to break that pattern. I'm going to teach you a better method of communication. So, I want you to see that we're not going to rehash any of your troubles. Instead, we're going to learn how to resolve them, and that's different!" "I'm just going to have to trust you, since Claire and I always end up worse off when we try to talk things out. We never get anywhere. She really doesn't listen to me at all," Philip muttered.

"Oh, yeah? You're always on my case about something! And you're right—I don't listen to that at all!" Claire retorted.

"Both of you take a deep breath and relax now," Dr. Brightman instructed comfortingly. "Philip, I understand you've been through quite a bout of depression. I'm sure you've been overwhelmed at work and with the situation at home. How have you been doing lately?"

"Well, thank you for asking, Doctor. As Claire may have told you, the bank where I work requested that I seek professional help. They suggested a psychiatrist—Dr. Sidney Bernard. So, I made an appointment and was evaluated for depression. My test showed a pretty high score. I had no idea I was depressed! I thought it was just a lot of stress I was feeling. But Dr. Bernard explained that I'm suffering from many symptoms of depression and recommended a two-fold approach of medication with counseling. He gave me a prescription for an antidepressant, which I've been taking, and he referred me to a counselor who has a lot of experience working with depression. Dr. Benjamin Graham is his name, and I've been seeing him for the last two months. Within about two weeks after starting the medication, I started feeling less depressed. I was also having trouble sleeping at night, so Dr. Bernard prescribed a mild sleeping aid which really helps me get the rest I need. So yeah—I'm in a better place for now," Philip related.

"I'm glad to hear you've found something that is working for you. You don't really seem depressed right now."

"Well, I guess you could say that I do feel depressed about the state of my marriage. Claire is so standoffish. She doesn't really believe I'll keep up with the therapy and taking the medication. She thinks I'll go back to my 'old, screwed up ways,' as she puts it. She keeps reminding me of all the mistakes she says I've made. I feel like I'm doing what I'm supposed to, but she is so resentful!" Philip griped. "I really don't want us to stay mired in this situation."

"I don't think either one of you wants to stay stuck like this. As you know, I've been working with Claire for the last several weeks. She, too, has obviously felt the impact of your depression. I'm going to explain to you what I've explained to her. **Depression is contagious, and what affects one spouse has a definite impact on the other.** She has experienced what we call 'situational depression.' Situational depression is a result of a prolonged and difficult situation that depletes a person's emotional resources. In turn, that person begins to develop maladaptive thinking and behaviors to cope with the situation. I call this '**Osmotic Depression**' because the environmental situation, like the process of osmosis, seeps into every fiber of their being. Osmosis is a process of biological absorption through cells in the body. Similarly, **those who live in contact with a depressed person absorb that depression.** You see, Philip, according to your doctor, your depression is different, and is most likely the result of a chemical imbalance. Claire, however, has developed **maladaptive behavior** to cope with your depressed state. She didn't understand what she was dealing with, and over time, she became depressed, as well. This combined situation has damaged your marriage, so neither of you has been able to function very well. At this point, I have to ask if both of you are willing to work on repairing your marriage."

"Well, I am," Claire responded immediately. "I've done a lot of work on myself, and I don't want to quit now."

Philip responded, "I don't know if things will ever be the same, and I really don't want to have to go through another separation and maybe even a divorce."

"Let's look at the situation and see what we can do. And, at this point, let's be optimistic about your chances for rebuilding your marriage," Dr. Brightman smiled.

"Let's check it out, then," Philip agreed, with a quick nod.

"You're experiencing what many couples experience. You've drifted apart, lost touch with each other, and have led rather independent lives. I'm sure you both have a lot of anger and frustration, as well as regrets and remorse. So, what I'm going to do is lay out a structure for you that we will use over the next few weeks to guide you through this process. I've worked with this process for seventeen years now, and it's been very effective. I'll explain the details to you as they come up in our future sessions."

"I'm really interested to hear more about this because I have no idea what to do next. We've been living in limbo," Claire stated flatly.

"Well, Doctor, I'm willing to listen to what you have to say, but I'll bet it's really going to take a lot of work. A whole lot of work! Claire's been so cold and distant and resentful toward me that it's hard to believe she can change. And the truth is,

I have a lot of resentment toward her too. She blames me for everything. So we're in sort of a holding pattern right now," Philip bit his words out in a clipped staccato.

"Well, that's what we need to change. To begin with, it is important that you declare a '**demilitarized zone**' in your home, meaning you should avoid discussion of your problems, just for now, to prevent any misunderstandings. We'll work on whatever problems come up in our sessions and learn skills to improve your communication. Alright?"

"How many sessions do you think this will take, Doctor?" Philip asked anxiously.

"It depends, but since you both have been in counseling and are doing well, I would say, maybe 8 to 10 sessions. This is solution-focused and not long-term counseling." She saw relief wash over their faces.

Working Through Feelings

"Welcome back, you two! Good to see you again," Dr. Brightman said and then began to present a platform for Claire and Philip to use as a basis for rebuilding their marriage. "We will start by working on improving **Communication skills**. There is a difference, you know, between talking and communicating. Communication involves listening and responding to create a meaningful dialog. Communication involves not only being heard, but also understanding what the other person is saying. Here are some handouts that explain this more."

"Philip usually just talks over me, or interrupts me, like it doesn't even matter if I understood what he said," Claire complained.

"Well, you probably weren't listening, anyway," Philip retorted, defensively.

"We'll continue to work on improving your communication," Dr. Brightman interjected. "But right now, I'd like to introduce something different. You both have spoken about your frustration and anger with each other. And I believe these past few months have been particularly rough. Sooner or later, these painful emotions will surface. So, I'm going to give you direction on what you need to do about that."

The counselor turned to Claire. "I'd like for you to put into words how Philip's depression affects you. You told me that living with depression took a terrible toll on you and your marriage. I want you to tell Philip what that's been like for you the past several months. I think Philip should hear your struggle."

Claire looked at Philip for a moment, and then began. "I felt so many things. I was so overwhelmed and felt helpless to do anything about it. I was confused and resentful. But the main feeling was a desire to leave! I wanted to run away and escape this mess of a marriage. I nearly did several times."

"You're telling him you were seriously thinking of ending your marriage because of this?" Dr. Brightman questioned.

"Yes, definitely!" Claire glared at Philip.

"Philip, you look shocked. Did you know Claire felt this way?"

"I had no idea it was that bad. I'm astounded!" Philip appeared to be blindsided. "I knew you weren't happy, but you never told me that you were thinking about leaving!" "I didn't think there was any way out of this," Claire said with frustration.

"What was the message you got from what she just said, Philip?" Dr. Brightman prompted.

"The message I got was that she really hates me!"

"Is that what you wanted him to hear?

"No. It's not that I hate you," she whispered. "But I did hate what we were going through and the confusion and resentment I felt. It was so overwhelming, and there was no solution that I could figure out, so I seriously considered leaving."

"Now, Philip, what does that say to you?"

"Well, it sounds like our marriage was in a lot worse shape than I thought," Philip looked dazed. "I was in a pretty bad state myself," he continued apologetically, "but according to you, I obviously failed. Claire, if things were that bad, maybe you should have left."

Dr. Brightman continued directing their dialogue. "I know this is hard for you, Philip, but if you can listen and understand, that's a critical step in connecting with her feelings. What else do you want to say to Claire?"

Blinking back his tears, Philip blurted out, "Claire, Honey, I'm so sorry. I was so caught up in my own misery and struggle that I didn't even notice what was happening to you. I felt like I was in a vacuum and didn't even care about myself. I was pretty empty, so I didn't have much to give anyway. I hear how it affected you, but I hope you can forgive me, and we can get past this. I love you, Claire, and I don't want to lose you."

The counselor noticed that Claire was now soaking tissue after tissue with tears. "What do you think Claire needs from you now, Philip? Do you want to ask her?"

"Yes! Claire, what can I do to help us get better?" "Hearing all you said meant a lot to me, Philip," Claire dabbed at her mascara, "I just need reassurance that you will continue to take your medications and keep your counseling appointments. It's obvious they've helped, and it will show me you are continuing to take care of yourself and your recovery."

"That's reasonable. I agree that's the right thing for me to do. I want to stay on the right track," Philip vowed.

"I know it was hard for both of you to stay focused and express these painful emotions," Dr. Brightman acknowledged.

"It was very hard. I had no idea what she was going through," Philip lowered his eyes, "and it has hurt me to hear it."

"It always hurts to hear of someone else's pain, but I want you to know this was a tremendously important session for both of you. I know you must feel drained. What do you need from me right now?" the doctor implored.

"I want to thank you so much for your support and encouragement in helping us get this far," Claire said, with a half-smile.

"Just keep us focused on improving our marriage and moving forward, Dr. Brightman."

"That I will do," Dr. Brightman assured. "Is this time next week still okay?" The couple agreed and then left, emotionally exhausted, but considerably less tense than when they had arrived.

From the Other Side

A week later, when Philip and Claire returned to Dr. Brightman's office, they were chatting quietly with one another, rather than maintaining their usual stony silence.

The doctor emerged from her office and greeted them. "Good to see you both again! Come on in, and let's get started. I almost hate to interrupt your exchange, but let's take a moment to catch up. You seem in better spirits today. How have things been going?"

"Well, as painful as it was, that last session really helped," Claire began. "Getting a lot of that garbage out was such a relief!"

"That's an understatement." Philip agreed. "I never realized what bad shape our marriage was in."

"That **processing skill** is what I'd like for you to use at home when feelings are running high. Follow the same structure we used in that session. I gave you some handouts to help you follow up on what we did," the doctor reminded them.

"You know, in our last session, I felt like that was the first time Philip really listened to me and understood where I was coming from," Claire said. "It made me feel so much better."

"And, I always feel better when Claire feels better."

"Philip, that's because you made a connection," Dr. Brightman noted.

Claire nodded. "Yeah, and that session really helped me understand more about Philip's struggle. I could actually sympathize with him, at least a little."

"Yes, and that reminds me... Philip," then Dr. Brightman asked. "Have you been able to process your own feelings in sessions with Dr. Bernard?"

"Well, sort of. But I'd like to be able to process like this with Claire," Philip said, leaning forward in his seat.

"I was hoping you'd say that."

"As Claire said, a lot of your personal struggle came out during our session last week," the counselor commented. "You talked about being in a pretty bad place yourself. So, I would like for you to process what that was like for you."

"Well," Philip began, "it was like I'd fallen into a black hole and couldn't get out. I knew something was wrong, but I thought I was just overwhelmed by stress. I couldn't relate to Claire at all because I felt she was always against me."

"That must have been very confusing and scary for you," the doctor noted. "It definitely was," Philip said dejectedly. "Everything seemed hopeless and futile. I just wanted to withdraw from everything and everybody—including Claire. I didn't even care about myself."

"What are you hearing, Claire?"

"That Philip didn't have much to give!" Claire turned towards Philip. "It sounds like you were running on empty."

"It seemed like everything in my life was going wrong, and I was angry about that. It was like everyone was against me—including you, Claire—and I just wanted to strike out."

"Is that what you did to Claire, Philip—strike out at her?" Dr. Brightman asked.

"Yes, unfortunately. She was the easiest target," he admitted.

"That did a lot of damage to you, didn't it, Claire?"

"I don't think you or anyone will ever know how much it affected me, Philip. It put me in a depressed state of my own."

"That's what depression does." The doctor noted. "It affects everyone involved—not just the depressed person. But unfortunately, it is not recognized as a major cause of conflict, or even divorce. It upsets the balance in a relationship. If left untreated, things become increasingly unbearable until one or the other will decide to give up and leave. That's why diagnosis, intervention, and treatment are so important."

"Then I guess it's a good thing after all that my boss intervened and gave me no option but to get evaluated," Philip said with resignation. "But I've never been so humiliated in my life! I wanted to give him a few choice words, stomp out of there, and never look back."

"That had to be hard to take, but you made the right choice, and I give you a lot of credit for that," Claire responded sympathetically.

"Thanks, for saying that, Claire. You can't imagine how threatening that was to me."

"That's a good way to put it," Dr. Brightman pointed out. "It actually was threatening, Philip. Your job and even your future were on the line. And I agree with Claire—it took a lot of courage for you to accept the challenge. I'm glad you overcame your pride and your impulse to leave and decided to seek answers."

"Yeah—it could have been a lot worse, believe me, if I had done what I really wanted to do!" Philip replied.

"Are you listening, Claire?"

"I never knew all this, Philip. You never told me how you really felt. I knew you were angry about being confronted by your boss, but I never realized how humiliating and shameful that was for you."

"Yeah—all of those bad feelings, and more—I hated myself for messing up. My self-esteem was on the floor," Philip confessed.

"That was a terrible day for you," Claire whispered.

"Just about the worst day ever. But when I heard you say you had intended to leave me I sank to a new level." Philip met Claire's eyes. "I had no idea that's where you were headed." "Do you feel now that you both have a better understanding of each other and what you each personally went through?"

"Yeah—this is pretty heavy, though," said Philip.

"Yes—it is heavy. But it's real," Dr. Brightman replied. "Maybe now you will be able to have more compassion and empathy for each other. Hopefully you can see how being more open, understanding and supportive will help you feel less isolated. The two of you took some pivotal steps today, and I want to stop right here today and let all this soak in. Next week, we'll work on this in some new ways."

Deciphering Coded Messages

The following week, Philip and Claire chatted amicably outside Dr. Brightman's office as they waited for their appointment.

"Welcome back," Dr. Brightman greeted them. "Come on in. Let's get caught up."

"Well, the last session made me feel like I'd been ripped open and my guts spilled out!" Philip groaned.

"I'm sure it did, but you really had to get that out," The doctor acknowledged.

"I know, but it took a few days for me to settle down. It did lift a burden, and it obviously helped Claire see what I was going through."

The doctor nodded. "Yes, she needed to hear that, and it helped you make an emotional connection with each other. I want that connection to grow. Now, I want to introduce another important relationship skill that fits into what we're talking about. So please listen; this is important: You know, we all have emotional needs. We're born dependent upon others for love, comfort, and care—it's in our DNA. If these needs are not met, a child will not thrive, and may not even survive. We don't outgrow these important emotional needs, either." Philip and Claire looked puzzled. Philip suddenly realized, "It makes us sound like a couple of whining children! Shouldn't we have enough grit and gall to function without a cheerleader?"

"I don't know, Philip," Claire interjected. "It would be nice to know that someone wants to cheer you on. Wasn't that one of your complaints—that your boss never gave you any praise or appreciation?"

"Yeah, he just always told me if there was a problem, I'd better take some action to straighten things out. He never seemed interested in anything else but the bottom line—just get the job done."

"So, Philip, you just made my point," the counselor observed. "You never received appreciation and validation to encourage you. We all need that. It's comforting to know that you have someone on your side. The Greek word for comfort means 'a calling to one's side,' and that's what we're talking about. **'I am for you and with you.'** We all have that ability to offer comfort and support. However, we often don't because we're unaware of how important this is to our emotional well-being. It's a buffer to stress.

Too often, a person is more invested in giving advice, making a judgment, or casting blame, rather than showing a compassionate response—basically, just being nurturing and kind in a time of need or stressful situation. When we receive that kind of emotional support, we feel cared for and loved. Without it we feel alone and disconnected from those we love," Dr. Brightman paused, looking to them for feedback.

Philip spoke first. "It sounds so simple, but you're right! I just never thought of putting it that way."

"You know, it's really a shame that we've never been able to do that for each other," Claire added sadly. "It's strange how far off we moved from something that should be so natural!"

"So, then we have this important element that we are missing in our relationships," Dr. Brightman continued, "even though it is a primary part of our human nature that cries out for attention. However, couples often speak in codes, and don't express these wants and needs directly. Instead of trying to understand and comfort one another, they sometimes use hostile attacks, criticisms, and blame to communicate their distress. For example, you hear complaints such as, 'You never do this,' or, 'You always do that,' or 'Why can't you _____?' Or, you'll receive a lecture saying that 'You need to do this,' or 'You should do that.' But remember, **what a person complains about the most is their point of greatest need. So, when you hear complaints or problems, you know that someone is expressing an unspoken need. The more complaining, the greater the need. What they're really asking for is understanding and support.** "By trying to reach out for some sort of emotional support, people may actually sabotage themselves by griping and complaining. Without realizing it, what they really want is emotional support and understanding. To help you realize what I'm saying, I'm going to give you some information that illustrates what this looks like. When your needs aren't met, you should say something like this:

1) **Need**: 'I'm really struggling, and I wish I could count on your support,' instead of, 'You never pay any attention. You just don't care!'

    Compassionate Response: 'I know you're going through a lot, and you shouldn't have to deal with this all by yourself. What do you need from me?' instead of, 'Gripe, gripe, gripe! That's all I ever hear from you!'

2) **Need**: 'This is really scary for me, and I don't know what to do. I need to know you're on my side,' instead of, 'You're always against me; you never take my side!'

    Compassionate Response: 'I don't want you to make a mistake, so let's figure this out together,' instead of, 'Well, you should have had all your ducks in a row by now.'

3) **Need**: 'This has been a difficult day. I'm exhausted, and I need a break,' instead of, 'I'm worn out, and you never help! There you are, just plopped down on the couch watching TV again!'

Compassionate Response: 'I know you've got a lot on your plate. Would you like for me to pick something up for dinner?' instead of, 'What about my day? I'm tired too, but I'm not whining and moaning about it like you!'

4) **Need**: 'I can't do this by myself; it's just too confusing. I need your input,' instead of, 'You always say you're going to help, but you never do.'

   Compassionate Response: 'Yeah, I can see how difficult this is. Maybe I can help,' instead of, 'Well, if you were better organized, it wouldn't be so confusing. You should have figured it out.'

5) **Need**: 'I'd like to be included in this and have you consider what I want, as well,' instead of saying, 'You're so selfish! All you want is to get your own way.'

   Compassionate Response: 'This is important, and I actually do value your opinion. Okay, what are your ideas?' instead of, 'If I wanted your opinion, I'd ask for it!'

6) **Need**: 'Let's be fair about our spending,' instead of, 'I'm sick of you complaining about my spending. What about all the money *you* spend?'

   Compassionate Response: 'What do you think is fair? We need to figure this out,' instead of, 'You're the one who's spending us into bankruptcy, so don't try to turn this around on me!'

7) **Need**: 'I need for you to listen and give me your attention,' instead of, 'You must be deaf! You never hear anything I say!'

   Compassionate Response: 'It sounds like you've got something important on your mind. So, go ahead. I'm listening,' instead of, 'If you didn't nag so much, maybe I would listen.'

8) **Need**: 'I'm really lonely and wish we could spend more time together,' instead of, 'You're always too busy and never have time for me.

Compassionate Response: 'Okay, let's make some plans. What do you want?' instead of, 'You're so demanding and bossy! Who wants to spend time with someone like that? Get a life.'

The doctor summed up: "Do you see the difference changing the language can make? The complaint disconnects us and creates blame. But when one expresses a **need**, it allows the other the chance to connect and show compassion. The message from one says, '**I have a need**,' while the response from the other says, '**I care!**' This is the language for responding to each other's emotional needs and establishing emotional intimacy. We depend upon each other for emotional support, from the smallest, most insignificant need to the major stressors of life. Sometimes we don't want to admit that," Dr. Brightman concluded.

"It's going to take a lot of practice to change all that," Philip commented. "But you're right. We just complain and gripe."

"Yeah, when I try to share a problem with Philip, I usually get a lecture. But that's definitely not what I need," Claire grumbled . "He just tells me what I should or shouldn't be doing."

"As you said, Philip, it's going to be a bit of a challenge for you both to remind yourselves to take a breather and remember that you need to let each other know that you care and are paying attention," Dr. Brightman summarized. "So, no matter what a person is going through, there's always an emotional edge to it. When we understand this and direct our language to the emotional content of the situation, we make a connection.. I want you to start working on making more of these emotional connections. Review the handouts I've given you. Try it, and you'll see that it makes a big difference."

"Sometimes I just feel the need to gripe," Philip honestly admitted.

"It's obvious that all of this is foreign to you," Claire huffed. "Remember when Dr. Brightman said that **if we keep doing what we're doing, we'll keep getting what we're getting?**"

"Are you needing reassurance that Philip really gets this and will follow through, Claire?" Dr. Brightman chided.

"Well—that would be nice for a change!"

"So, why don't you use the language that will elicit his reassurance?"

"Oh, I get what you're doing," Claire replied, looking embarrassed. "Philip, I'd feel much better if you reassured me that you understand this, and you'll follow through."

"I'm not perfect, but I can promise you, Claire, that I will make a definite effort. I hope you will, too," he replied, as they walked together toward the door together.

Mending and Blending

"Welcome back, you two," Dr. Brightman greeted. "Let's take a moment to hear what's happening regarding depression. Then we'll talk about emotional support. Claire, why don't you begin today?"

"Well, I have to say that I think we're both leaving the depression behind. Philip's supervisor even complimented him this week on his attitude. It made me very proud to hear that, and Philip isn't as critical and negative about everything I do. He's a lot more patient than he used to be. He's more upbeat now when we talk, and that's been a huge relief."

"I'm feeling a lot more optimistic about our marriage and my own future," Philip added. "Things aren't perfect, but we're moving forward. I need to refill my medication soon. It's hard to admit that I need a pill to feel better, but I know that it does help. On a brighter note, we've been enjoying some really good times together!" "I didn't realize how we'd forgotten to enjoy each other and have fun until we started these sessions," Claire commented with a grin.

"Okay! This is good news. So, how about some feedback on emotional intimacy? Back to you, Claire."

"I've been reading the information you gave us, trying to absorb it. I know I have some bad habits to break, and those handouts help. It's so easy to gripe and complain, but I'm making an effort to bite my tongue and think before I speak."

"Yeah, but you could use a little more effort," Philip teased.

"Thanks a lot, Philip. You know, you're not much better! You should be grateful for what you get."

"Here we go again!" Dr. Brightman interjected. "Neither of you sound very caring and considerate at the moment."

Claire agreed. "Okay. You can see we still need a lot of practice. Hey, where are my handouts when I need them!"

"Don't worry. It takes time to form new habits. Just remember, practice makes perfect. You will see how things calm down when you remember to address the need instead of launching complaints."

"Absolutely. But there's something else I want to say to Claire." Philip paused and turned to her. "If you still want to start your own practice, I want you to know I'll support you as best I can. I know it's what you've always wanted, and it's not too late. I don't want to be a dream killer."

"Do you really mean that? I have put those plans on the shelf for a long time!"

"I really do, Claire. And now I get to be the hero. Right, Dr. Brightman?"

"You got that right! I know it's a good feeling after seeing yourself in such a negative light," Dr. Brightman agreed. This does give you a chance to shine in Claire's eyes. So, keep up the good work!"

"Yeah, I want you to be my hero again, Philip!" Claire exclaimed. "Sometimes I need you to rescue me."

"Now, let me go over what we've worked on together,' the counselor summarized. "You have learned better **communication skills**. You've seen how important it is to enjoy **shared good times** on a regular basis. You have learned how to **process feelings**, and now you've learned how to make an **emotional connection.** So, I will predict something else: Your **physical intimacy** will naturally result from these ongoing emotional connections. If you continue to build on what you've learned here, you won't need me anymore, will you?" Dr. Brightman chuckled.

"You will need to continue with your medication though, Philip, until your doctor either modifies or discontinues it. I think this session concludes everything we set out to accomplish together. I'd like to release you for the time being, but anytime you need a tune up, you can come back in for a refresher."

"Yes, Doctor, it's been an uphill climb, and we'll keep climbing, I hope," Philip spoke. "I don't ever want to go back to the way we were."

"Thank you so much, Dr. Brightman." Claire added. "You've helped us so much. Without you, we would probably be divorced by now. I really had no hope of things ever getting better. I don't see how we could ever have untangled all of this."

"With your help, we both feel like we've accomplished quite a bit," Philip nodded. "We appreciate all you've done!"

• • •

Postscript

- Osmotic Depression is depression attributed to prolonged exposure to a clinically depressed person. Osmotic depression is absorbed from the pathological environment in which the healthy individual lives. The unconscious maladaptation of coping, along with defense mechanisms in order to survive this erratic and toxic life is characteristic of this type of depression. It is experienced as "crazy making." That is, the people living in the "crazy" world of the depressed begin to feel crazy themselves.

- Unhealthy people make healthy people sick.
- Depression is different for many men, and the symptoms are particularly shameful because they feel weak, inadequate, vulnerable, insecure, and helpless to handle these feelings. They often lash out in anger and rage at their preferred target. Men want help, but vigorously defend any suggestion or offer. They withdraw, avoid contact and stonewall any discussion about their symptoms, seemingly unaware of the impact they're having. A man's lack of awareness of his own needs often causes him to shift the blame for his misery onto his partner and attack her for his presumed failures. When confronted, his emotions may escalate rapidly, hoping to scare off anyone who would attempt to hold him accountable.

What you need to know about depressed persons

They may have a combination of these symptoms, but not necessarily all of them:

- They are self-absorbed. They don't notice the impact they have on you.
- They are emotionally unstable, exhibiting an up and down roller coaster of feelings.
- They believe their problems are caused by other people or situations, rather than by their own negative beliefs.
- They put you on the defensive with their accusations and interrogations.
- They are critical of what you do, even though you are trying to please them.
- They are extremely sensitive to how you treat them, but they are insensitive to how they treat you.
- They become angry and resent offers of help.

- They are incongruent; that is, their words and actions don't match. They say one thing but do the opposite.
- They are distracted and don't finish what they start.
- They hoard and live with clutter.
- They have a tendency to medicate with alcohol, drugs, or food, and that often leads to a problem with weight.
- They lack energy and motivation.
- They sleep more than necessary.
- They complain of frequent aches and pains.
- They are unpredictable—agreeable and compliant one minute, adversarial and hostile the next.
- They are forgetful, particularly when they don't want to remember something.
- They project their negative, pessimistic outlook onto everything and everyone.

What to Notice about Depression

What are your alternatives if you live with a depressed person?

Try to encourage that person to get help. Antidepressant medication is often helpful to stabilize moods and therapy to help learn better coping mechanisms and relationship skills.

You might:

- Live a life of quiet desperation (becoming depressed yourself).
- Live an independent life, pursuing personal interests and activities.
- Leave and get a life of your own.
- Engage in marriage/relationship therapy, if the depressed person is willing.

Symptoms of Osmotic Depression

You may have many, but not necessarily all of these symptoms:

- I question my own sanity.
- I'm always "walking on eggshells."
- I feel guilty when I don't measure up to impossible standards.
- I'm constantly on the defensive.
- I've lost my self-esteem due to criticism and blame.
- I have more stress-related health problems.
- I'm increasingly angry and frustrated.
- I seek escapes through alcohol or substances, or food.
- I seriously think of leaving my relationship.
- I feel exhausted, even when rested.
- I have difficulty concentrating on required tasks.
- I believe the worst about myself.
- I keep trying harder and harder with no results.
- I fear my partner's anger and threats.
- I feel like I've lost myself.
- I keep thinking things will get better.
- I'm afraid to speak out.
- I wear a mask and play a part.
- I feel "scapegoated" most of the time.
- I feel lonely and abandoned.
- I get confused about right and wrong.
- I feel unlovable and unworthy.
- I've developed a hard shell to protect myself.
- I look for outside sources of happiness.
- I am vulnerable to an affair.
- I'm discouraged about ever getting what I want or need.
- I feel trapped and helpless.
- I have trouble sleeping or sleep too much.
- I don't care about things I used to care about.

How You Are Treated

You are:

- Constantly put down.
- Constantly blamed for his/her mistakes and problems.
- Condemned and criticized for every real or imagined flaw.
- Accused of things you never thought or did.
- The target of his/her distorted thinking.
- Expected to be perfect, and criticized when you are not.
- Expected to please him/her or suffer the consequences.
- Questioned about every choice or decision you make.
- Resisted when you want or need something.
- Regarded as the problem.
- Scolded and lectured.
- Ignored and discounted.
- Beginning to believe his/her distortions, particularly those about you.
- Berated about your family/friends or anything you enjoy.
- Beginning to develop health issues.
- Treated unfairly.
- Treated like an inconvenience and a bother.
- Put in 'no-win' situations.

Depression

Depression is a mood disorder that impacts a person's daily life. It may be described as feelings of sadness, loss, or anger; feelings of hopelessness, or despair that won't go away. Some describe days as "living in a black hole" having a feeling of impending doom, feeling empty, lifeless, and apathetic. Men in particular feel angry, and are restless and irritable.

10 Common Symptoms:

1) Feeling helpless and hopeless. A dark outlook. Nothing will ever get better. And nothing I can do will change the situation.

2) Loss of interest in regular activities. Nothing is enjoyable that once was. Inability to feel joy or pleasure.

3) Appetite or weight changes. Either weight loss or weight gain—a change of more than 5% per month.

4) Sleep changes—either inability to sleep or sleeping too much.

5) Anger or irritability—feeling agitated, restless, or hostile and violent. Low tolerance, short temper—everything and everyone gets on your nerves.

6) Loss of energy—feeling fatigued, physically drained, body feels like carrying a heavy burden. Small tasks are exhausting and take longer to complete.

7) Self-loathing—strong feelings of worthlessness, or harshly criticizing yourself for perceived faults or mistakes.

8) Reckless behavior—engaging in escapist behaviors. Potential for substance abuse, impulsiveness, reckless driving or dangerous sports.

9) Concentration problems—trouble focusing, making decisions, or remembering.

10) Unexplained aches or pains—increase in physical complaints such as headaches, back pain, achy muscles, stomach aches, digestive problems.

Depression/Suicide Risk:

- Talk of killing or harming oneself.
- Strong feelings of despair or feeling trapped.
- Unusual preoccupation with death or dying.
- Acting recklessly (as if with a death wish).

- Calling or visiting people to say good-bye.
- Getting affairs in order—giving away prized possessions.
- Saying things like "everyone would be better off without me."
- Sudden shift from being extremely depressed to acting calm and happy.

Be Your Own Best Friend

1) **Stop all self-criticism**—When you criticize yourself, you create negative emotions and internal distress inside yourself. When you forgive yourself and reconcile with yourself, you create positive emotions.

2) **Don't scare yourself**—Stop terrorizing yourself with catastrophic thinking. When you think the worst, you create inner anxiety. Switch your focus to positive, optimistic thoughts. Look at the glass as half full, not half empty.

3) **Be kind, gentle, and patient with yourself**—Give yourself a break and treat yourself with consideration. You are probably doing the best you can at the moment. If you don't respect yourself, who will?

4) **Praise yourself**—Give yourself a personal pat on the back when you take a step forward. Encourage yourself and celebrate your progress.

5) **Support yourself**—Make a commitment to self-development and personal growth. Seek supportive relationships and allow others to support your progress.

6) **Learn your own personal limits**—We all have limits to what we can give. Know when your time, efforts, energy has gone far enough. Know when you have reached your financial limits. Know when and how to say NO.

7) **Avoid people who are troublemakers**—unless you want trouble. Don't think you can change them; you can't. You can only change yourself by getting out of their way.

Vocabulary List of Feelings

SAD	ANGRY	FEAR
Frustrated	Overwhelmed	Trapped
Lonely	Hostile	Scared
Vulnerable	Furious	Panicked
Confused	Annoyed	Anxious
Withdrawn	Irritated	Nervous
Empty	Resentful	Concerned
Drained	Bitter	Afraid
Lost	Disgusted	Threatened
Discouraged	Appalled	Desperate
Disappointed	Agitated	Helpless
Bored	Upset	Hindered
Sad	Tired of	Torn
Hurt	Offended	Smothered
Crushed	Ignored	Blocked
Used	Envious	Conflicted
Unappreciated	Bothered	Burdened
Rejected	Irate	Suspicious
Neglected	Mad	Cautious
Hopeless	Vengeful	Jealous
Abused	Combative	Embarrassed
Grieved	Aggressive	Intimidated
Ashamed	Rude	Humiliated
Guilty	Resistant	Abandoned
Defeated		Terrified